"In *Letters to an Appre*
ferro provides both a p
challenge for every Chi
the lives of others. After riding the dusty roads of Uganda with Jeremy, walking through refugee settlements with him, and watching him interact with his children, his team members, and indigenous church leaders, I can testify to the fact that Jeremy is modeling what he encourages his readers to do. I can also state that his book has inspired and equipped me to be a better mentor. I highly recommend it."

—**Paul Chitwood**,
President, International Mission Board, SBC

"This is a unique book on organic mentoring. The author, who has had vast missionary experience, has been ministered to by devoted mentors during crucial times in his life. The letters from the mentors as well as the insights of the author can provide significant guidance and encouragement for mentors as well as mentorees. As the author's former professor, I can assure you that your life will be truly blessed and you will be seriously challenged as you read this marvelous book."

—**Daniel R. Sánchez**,
Distinguished Professor of Missions,
Southwestern Baptist Theological Seminary

"I would consider myself a man who had only one mentor who took an active interest in me. Much of my growth in the faith happened in spite of, not because of, other Christians, or so I thought.

The one person I thought was my only mentor was Bob Roberts Jr., who took me under his wing and taught me church multiplication and engaging the world. Now Bob continues to teach me how to be a Christian in the public square and engage other faiths.

After reading Jeremy's book, I realize I am the product of many mentors of many kinds from a distance, and I am encouraged to live even more on purpose and even closer to other young men to be more intentional with them.

But what could happen through me if I was even more intentional? Jeremy has given inspiration and some very practical principles on being a Paul and a Timothy. He has written a moving account of how men and women have shaped his life, and I'm motivated to live like those mentors. I love this book!"

—**Mitchell Jolly**,
Founder, Teaching Pastor at Three Rivers Church, Rome, Georgia

"I learned something on every page! At times, it seemed like the letters were written to me. Whether you're in a mentor role or an apprentice role, the examples and wisdom in this book can help propel you and those around you toward Jesus."

—**Clayton Bullion**,
BSM Director at Tarleton State University,
Cofounder of Campus Multiplication Network

"Mentoring is about relationships—and relationships are about people. God often gives us the gift of people in our lives so we might become more like Him through their influence and witness. This book is a testament to that fact. It introduces you to many of Jeremy's mentors while also fervently and practically challenging you to find a mentor and be one, too. I have mentored several men, but this book has pushed me to think even more intentionally about how I do it."

—Dr. Chuck Lawless,
Dean of Doctoral Studies and VP for Spiritual Formation,
Southeastern Baptist Theological Seminary

"*Letters to an Apprentice: A Culture of Mentorship* is a refreshing reminder that the best mentoring happens in the trenches. Classrooms, training centers, and coffee shops are no substitute for side-by-side, real-life, boots-on-the-ground experiences in the context of a significant relationship. I wholeheartedly recommend this book because it inspires us to pursue godly, "one another" relationships and gives real-life examples of how God uses those relationships to transform one's mind and heart. *Letters to an Apprentice* is a powerful reminder of the need to be mentored and to mentor, and I have seen firsthand how J lives out the lessons found in this book."

—Daren Davis,
Affinity Leader, sub-Saharan Africa, IMB

"Jeremy has lived out mentorship for decades in the Amazon jungle and the African bush, modeling biblical discipleship as he shares the gospel and his life as well. In this book, Jeremy blesses readers with the stories, lessons, and relationships the Lord used to grow him in the faith, and how these all became examples for him on what true mentorship looks like. Jeremy revives a form of mentorship that values character, honesty, transparency, accountability, and truth. At a time when many relationships seem to lack such values, Jeremy's book comes at just the right time in hopes of casting a refreshed and timeless vision of organic mentorship that seeks true transformation."

—**Jonathan Williams**,
Senior Pastor of Wilcrest Baptist Church, Houston, Texas,
Author, *Gospel Family: Cultivating Family Discipleship,
Family Worship, & Family Missions*

"One of the greatest needs in the church is hands-on, relational mentorship and life and ministry training, and Jeremy has spent two decades in ministry pursuits that relied on this level of mentorship. I appreciate the candid language, clear examples, and real-life stories of how mentorship can be and has been accomplished. In an age where the ability to connect relationally is being diminished by social media, electronic correspondence, and failed mentorship in the home, Jeremy nails it. This book is both timely and relevant, but it is also timeless and principled. We needed this."

—**Brody Holloway,**
Cofounder and Lead Pastor of Snowbird Wilderness Outfitters,
Teaching Pastor of Red Oak Church, Andrews, North Carolina

LETTERS TO AN APPRENTICE

A CULTURE OF MENTORSHIP

J. TALIAFERRO

LUCIDBOOKS

Letters to an Apprentice
A Culture of Mentorship

Copyright © 2020 by J. Taliaferro

Published by Lucid Books in Houston, TX
www.LucidBooksPublishing.com

Unless otherwise indicated, all Scripture quotations are taken from the Holman Christian Standard Bible®, Copyright © 1999, 2000, 2002, 2003, 2009 by Holman Bible Publishers. Used by permission. HCSB® is a federally registered trademark of Holman Bible Publishers.

Scripture quotations marked (ESV) are taken from the ESV® Bible (The Holy Bible, English Standard Version®), copyright © 2001 by Crossway, a publishing ministry of Good News Publishers. Used by permission. All rights reserved.

Scripture quotations marked (NASB) are taken from the New American Standard Bible® (NASB), Copyright © 1960, 1962, 1963, 1968, 1971, 1972, 1973, 1975, 1977, 1995 by The Lockman Foundation. Used by permission. www.Lockman.org.

Scripture quotations marked (NIV) are taken from the Holy Bible, New International Version®, NIV®. Copyright ©1973, 1978, 1984, 2011 by Biblica, Inc.™ Used by permission of Zondervan. All rights reserved worldwide. www.zondervan.com The "NIV" and "New International Version" are trademarks registered in the United States Patent and Trademark Office by Biblica, Inc.™

eISBN: 978-1-63296-394-9
ISBN: 978-1-63296-487-8

Special Sales: Most Lucid Books titles are available in special quantity discounts. Custom imprinting or excerpting can also be done to fit special needs. Contact Lucid Books at Info@LucidBooksPublishing.com.

Dedicated to Marietta Houston, my great-grandmother and very first mentor. With just a simple chalkboard in her kitchen, she taught me as a young child how to memorize scripture. She made it all so relevant and life-giving. That is the essence of mentorship.

TABLE OF CONTENTS

Foreword	xi
Preface: A Call to Action	xiii
Introduction to Organic Mentorship	1
Chapter 1: A Word to the Wise: Draw from Many Wells	5
Chapter 2: Foundations	11
Bill and Nadine Taliaferro: Faithfulness, Perseverance, and Hard Work	12
Dr. Jack Dale: Stepping out of Your Comfort Zone	15
Chapter 3: Preparation	19
Jeff Glenn: Finding Identity	20
Jesse Fletcher: Man's Greatest Endeavor	23
James Shields: Serious-Mindedness	26
Linda Carleton: Learning to Listen	29
Chapter 4: To the Nations	33
Chris Ammons: Love the Church	34
Avery Willis: Prepare for a Helpmate	38
Steve King: Mobilized to the Nations	42
Randy Griffin: Capable and Humble	46
Jerry Rankin: Protect Your Flock	51
David Payne: Worthy Communication	56

Chapter 5: Starting Over	61
Tim Cearley: Tell Them about Jesus	62
Dr. Bob Calvert: Drive On	67
Kevin Rodgers: Trusting Sovereignty	70
Chapter 6: The Missing Chapter: A Difficult Question	75
Chapter 7: Developing a Culture of Mentorship	79
Chapter 8: Dear Paul: Invest in the Future	83
Chapter 9: Dear Timothy: Choose Wisely	89
Chapter 10: A Starting Point and a Path Forward	95
Epilogue	101
Acknowledgments	109

FOREWORD

I watched Jeremy before I knew him. I was told by those I trusted we were cut from the same cloth. I wanted to know if that was true, so I set about doing my due diligence to confirm or deny what I had heard. Jeremy was working in the Amazon at the time, taking young people under his wing as he led them to the edge and beyond. While it was easy to see that Jeremy took his team members beyond civilization and the typical comforts and conveniences of most South American mission trips, it was the pieces that you could not easily see that so impressed me. It was how Jeremy took his team members and volunteers to the edge of endurance and personally demonstrated how to let Christ be strong when they were so weak. It was how he took a person who had cried the call of Isaiah—"Here am I, Lord, send me"—in a comfortable pew to a place where they could see God working in the midst of desperation, hardship, and pain. It was a place where many average Christians may have well cried out "My God, my God, why have You forsaken me?" But it was at that very place where his team members were challenged to get out of the boat and join Jesus on the rough seas of desperation to see where God was most at work in both the indigenous as well as those who went to serve. Vetting complete.

As Jeremy was serving the Lord in South America, I was running a ministry called Fusion. Our ministries had a similar penchant and ethos for godly obedience only found through an organic, life-on-life mentorship forged through hardship, defined by discipline, and empowered by a personal commitment to Christ. The success of these relationships was not found in comfort or success, but godly obedience. It was life-on-life learning that could never be taught in the classroom. We were, indeed, cut from a similar cloth.

I was to find, when we finally met in East Africa in 2015, that our lives, though different, were guided by a similar creed. I watched him pour into his Journeymen who were giving two years of their lives to take the gospel to some of the darkest and most dangerous places in Africa. I watched as he taught them biblical storying. Held them accountable to the study and memorization of God's Word, and trained them to survive and thrive in the bush as they lived and shared gospel with all who would listen. I watched as he exemplified the words of the Fusion Creed:

As a follower of Christ, I am not called to comfort or success, but to obedience. Consequently, my life is to be defined not by what I do but by who I am.

Henceforth, I will proclaim His name without fear, follow Him without regret, and serve Him without compromise.

Thus, to obey is my objective, to suffer is expected, His glory is my reward.

Therefore, to Christ alone be all honor, all power, and all glory that the world may know.

Amen.

Jeremy truly reflects these words in his ministry, in his family, and his life. Thank you, Jeremy, for your godly example to me and so many others. Thank you for fulfilling the Great Commission while demonstrating the Greatest Commandment: so others may hear… and live!

Rev. Scott A. Brawner,
Fusion Founder,
President, Concilium Inc.

PREFACE
A CALL TO ACTION

For Paul and Timothy

I want to start this endeavor by helping you understand why I am writing this book. I have had an amazing journey of mentorship throughout my life, and I want everyone to have access to life-changing mentors like I have had.

However, that doesn't just happen. First, you must learn to recognize what is around you. You might find you already have a mentor speaking into your life, but maybe you have not recognized them for who they are and are not taking full advantage of the relationship.

You may be involved in a mentorship program that is not giving you the fulfillment you expected or hoped for. The people involved are almost always well intentioned and truly desire to see you grow. But having never been organically mentored themselves, they don't know how to produce it in others. So they are left to rely on less productive and less fulfilling forms of mentorship. Both forms can bear good fruit, but only one will produce a lasting result that affects multiple generations and can even change the world.

So let's start with clear definitions.

A Tale of Two Seeds: Heirloom or Hybrid?

Organic mentorship is a passing on of knowledge, passions, and lifestyles through relational means. Most of these relationships are life on life, meaning your lives are bumping into each other regularly, often in very informal ways. These mentorship relationships can take place over long periods of time, but they can even happen during short encounters if the apprentice is open and ready to learn and be influenced toward new areas of growth.

Organic mentorship is like planting a tomato plant with an heirloom seed. After the harvest of the previous year, you set aside some of the seeds from the nicest tomatoes and save them to plant next year. You do that year after year, and the tomatoes get better and better. Also, the farmer who uses heirloom seeds never runs out of seeds because he relies on the previous harvest to provide for the next season. In the same way, organic mentorship requires reproducibility. It is deeply dependent on one generation passing on its knowledge, passion, and lifestyle to the next generation.

Organizational mentorship is teaching information and knowledge through organized processes and checklists. This style of mentorship is usually led by chosen teachers or mentors who have an impressive amount of knowledge but may have no natural connection with the apprentice.

Organizational mentorship is akin to planting a tomato plant with hybrid seeds you buy from the store. Those seeds are genetically engineered to produce the biggest, reddest tomatoes. They look amazing on your Instagram account. The desirable features are all there, and everyone is jealous of your garden, but the actual taste lacks the depth of the heirloom tomato. And every year, the farmer has to buy new seeds because hybrid plants produce sterile seeds. They cannot be used the next year.

Before we completely throw out organizational mentorship, we must recognize that it has its place. It works well when training people to safely do a task; it is effective in schools and addiction programs. But its biggest flaw is that it cannot pass on knowledge from generation to generation because the information did not penetrate deeply into the day-to-day life of the apprentice.

Most companies, churches, and organizations focus on the organizational style of mentorship because they can produce the "Wow!" factor. Hybrid seeds (organizational mentorship) produce prize pumpkins that weigh 800 pounds and win prizes even though they taste terrible. But everybody knows the best produce comes from the multigenerational garden of the old farmer who has been using heirloom seeds (organic mentorship) that have been passed down season after season.

Organic vs. Organizational Growth

Mentorship can take many forms. Unfortunately, over the years, the term has become dry and uninspiring—perhaps mostly because we have tried to institutionalize it. We have tried to turn mentorship into a program instead of letting it happen in the context of a deep, organic relationship.

We assign people mentors instead of letting their relationships naturally produce the mentor-apprentice role. We require mentors to write reports and give a grade for their apprentices' growth instead of letting God's timing guide their timeline.

What God initially intended was one passionate disciple inspiring and leading the next generation into a passionate pursuit of Christ. Yet we have settled for passing on information or ethos without the passion that drives us to submit to the painful process of sanctification.

Organizational mentorship is education-based and primarily concerned with the information required to master a topic. It is very scholastic, and although it can be done outside of a school, it seems most at home with an open book and a curious mind. It is more concerned with understanding than actions. It wants to know you can grasp the material and perform the task, but it is less concerned whether you live in such a way that you are completely consumed by the topic.

Organic mentorship, on the other hand, is relational and experience-based. Education is important, but information must be grounded in real life for it to take root.

Imagine this: Five hundred years ago, if you wanted to learn to be a blacksmith, you would go and live with the local smitty. You would come to love the smell of coal and wake in the morning to the sound of the forge and bellows. Your body would change as your hands and arms grew stronger. You would learn to read the color of the metal to learn when and how to strike the hammer, when to put the metal back into the forge, and when to quench. You would eat what a blacksmith eats and drink what a blacksmith drinks. You would learn smitty jokes—and probably grow an amazing mustache! You would have scars from slag and burns from unwittingly grabbing hot metal. Living the life of a blacksmith is not just swinging a hammer. You must understand the material, perform the task, *and* live the lifestyle.

In the same way, the church is an organic form of life that should reproduce itself in organic ways. That is how you see things passed on in the Bible. Someone who knew scripture was responsible for mentoring a younger disciple and passing on not only the information but also the life of a disciple.

In the Old Testament, Moses mentored Joshua and Caleb. He identified them and then invited them to be by his side. They were there during trials, they listened as he made big decisions, they upheld him in his times of weakness or need, and ultimately, they continued the work he started as they crossed the River Jordan with the Israelites.

Elijah trained Elisha. He taught him how to hear the word from the Lord and how to proclaim truth to the people of God. He prepared him for the life of a prophet, which can be very dangerous and lonely.

A CALL TO ACTION

In Proverbs, a father instructs his son in the way he should live. He teaches him about wisdom and discipline. Be assured that those things were not only taught with written words; they were taught first by actions and then reinforced by the written word.

In the New Testament, the paradigm continues. It is a bit different since a new character—Holy Spirit—is introduced (though He had always been, He had never played such an obvious role). First, Jesus mentored a diverse and unsuspecting group of men and women for three years before his death. Later, the veil of the Temple was torn asunder, and the Spirit of God saw fit to make His dwelling place in people—and everything changed!

These very practical mentor relationships became supercharged because there was another mentor introduced: the Holy Spirit. He is our counselor and ever-present help in time of trouble. He doesn't make mistakes as a mentor would but empowers each mentor to walk the apprentice into new life.

For three years, Jesus walked with His disciples. They slept in the same place, traveled the same paths, and ate the same food. He taught them the ways of the kingdom of God, and He corrected their mistakes in a patient yet uncompromising fashion. They didn't even know what was happening to them, but Jesus was preparing them for the task they had been called to, and it would all come together in due time.

Jesus taught them about the body life—how to live together as the Body of Christ and how to care for one another and spread the truth to the world. And when He left, He gave them His Spirit to guide them and help them know the proper path.

Barnabas took Paul as his apprentice, and they became co-laborers. Then Paul chose Silas, Timothy, Titus, and others and passed on to them the things he had learned.

Peter took on John Mark and mentored him by teaching him the things he had learned while following Jesus. In fact, John Mark helped Peter pen those things into the Gospel of Mark. Every mentor has his or her own way of passing on the wisdom and teachings of Christ. There is not only one way. Be creative! Let God use you in the unique way He made you.

Organic mentorship (as opposed to a more formal and scholastic teacher-student role) helps keep the integrity of the teacher's words because of the respect garnered for the mentor in the day-to-day relationship. The passing on of practical and spiritual wisdom gives apprentices a more advanced starting place. They get a head start in their spiritual development because they trust the experience of their mentor. And to some degree, they desire to live like the mentor. Because of the relationship and history, they are emboldened to try things and take risks they normally would not take, mostly because they have already seen the benefit play out in the mentor's life.

That speeds up the maturing of God's people, which is greatly needed today. Most Christians mature at such a slow rate that the Body of Christ stagnates. It compromises our mission in the world because we have no one mature enough to fulfill tasks the way God intended.

I have been in many churches both overseas and in the United States where the problems in the church were because the church had no true elders who fit the character traits from 1 Timothy 3 and Titus 1. A lack of elders stems from our departure from biblical mentorship. It is time we recognize that the educational and scholastic form of discipleship is not producing the leaders we need to guide us.

We don't need smart or well-informed leaders, but we need leaders who have godly character and love to pass on to the younger generation the joys of being a disciple.

It's time we make a change for our own good but also, more importantly, for the sake of the kingdom and the calling we were given to take the good news of Jesus to every nation.

So what should we do? Let's revive that ancient form of mentorship! It was the backbone of true transformation and sanctification

A CALL TO ACTION

in scripture. The early Christians grew because of the community they were committed to and how they invested in one another.

I'm hoping to stir within you a desire for something deeper. I also want to stoke within you the desire to have someone speak into your life, to offer you wisdom and guidance—a friend you respect and love deeply who can help you develop into the man or woman of God you were meant to be. But I also want to inspire you to teach others what you have learned on the path God has taken you. I want you to have an organic desire to reproduce in the lives of others the fruit God has given you in your life.

INTRODUCTION TO ORGANIC MENTORSHIP[1]

The one who walks with the wise will become wise, but a companion of fools will suffer harm.
—Prov. 13:20

Two are better than one because they have a good reward for their efforts. For if either falls, his companion can lift him up; but pity the one who falls without another to lift him up.
—Eccles. 4:9–10

---

1. I want to take this opportunity to make the distinction between discipleship and mentorship. I would characterize discipleship as a primarily spiritual endeavor, focused on biblical understanding and spiritual life. Mentorship is larger than that, and though it includes the same spiritual aspects, it also speaks into daily life, marriage, work, child-rearing, attitudes, and such.

Elijah and Elisha, Eli and Samuel, Jesus and the disciples, Barnabas and Paul, Paul and Timothy, Peter and John Mark—all these people shared in an extraordinary relationship called mentorship. When an older disciple who has walked with the Lord and developed wisdom and character takes a young believer as a disciple or apprentice, something very special happens. The passing on of truth from one generation to the next has been part of the Christian experience since the first century. In fact, it was the original way the church passed on doctrinal understanding and taught future generations what it meant to be found in Christ.

> *And what you have heard from me in the presence of many witnesses, commit to faithful men who will be able to teach others also.*
> —2 Tim. 2:2

It also was a vital part of the Jewish culture in the Old Testament. God's command to His people in Deuteronomy centered on the idea that we must pass on—to each new generation in a personal and relational way—our knowledge about the Creator and what He requires of us.

> *Listen, Israel: The LORD our God, the LORD is One. Love the LORD your God with all your heart, with all your soul, and with all your strength. These words that I am giving you today are to be in your heart. Repeat them to your children. Talk about them when you sit in your house and when you walk along the road, when you lie down and when you get up. Bind them as a sign on your hand and let them be a symbol on your forehead. Write them on the doorposts of your house and on your gates.*
> —Deut. 6:4–9

INTRODUCTION TO ORGANIC MENTORSHIP

Though the written Word is sufficiently powerful and authoritative for an individual's spiritual growth, nothing can match the impact of life experiences being passed on from an elder to a younger believer who desires to know the path of Christ.

That has been my experience. From my childhood, there has rarely been a moment when I did not have a mentor profoundly speaking into my life. I can safely say that these men and women made me who I am today. This book is just a creative telling of that story.

The letters you are about to read were not actually written by my mentors. It is just a way for me to compile what each one of them taught me into a short but personal format. I will share the nuggets of wisdom they gave me, the teachings that discipled me through hard times, and the foundations they gave me on which to build my future. As much as possible, I try to write in their voice or at least how I remember them so you can get a sense of how God used very different people in my life to accomplish His purposes.

Some mentors have been in my life for a long time; others came and went. Some I learned from by walking through life together; others I watched from afar. But they all impacted me in some way—and it was all significant.

This book is in chronological order because the progression of growth is significant. The Lord does not expect us to be perfect all at once, but He sends these special people into our lives to guide us through the obstacles at a specific time. He doesn't need to see perfection but rather obedience and progress. That is how mentors challenge us every day. Sometimes, when we look back, we are ashamed of what we did in the past, for our naivete or lack of wisdom. But I have learned to be content that I was faithful with what I was entrusted with and that I was being obedient with what I understood at that point in my life. Thankfully, I know better now than I knew then, mostly because of the mentors God placed in my life.

The purpose of this book is twofold. My first desire is to encourage you to submit yourself to mentorship. I want to inspire you to seek it out because of the benefit it will be to both you and your local church body. I want you to see an example of what happens to you as you are mentored through the different stages of development so you will look for the right men and women to guide and direct you as you walk through life.

Second, this book was written to urge you to pay it forward. I always tell those I mentor that the only thing I require from them is that they take someone under their wing at the proper time and mentor them. I urge them to pass on the things they have learned from me and others. In effect, this book is a guide for you to become a Paul and a Timothy, a mentor and an apprentice.

CHAPTER 1
A WORD TO THE WISE: DRAW FROM MANY WELLS

Let's say Mike finds a water well. He really likes the taste of the water from that well, so he draws only from that well for years and years. After a while, Mike begins to think water is only supposed to taste like the water from his well. Any other taste means the water is bad. The other water actually may be totally acceptable; it is just different. Some wells may be sweeter or have more minerals, but Mike will never know because he has a very narrow view of what water truly is. He doesn't know much about water; he only knows *his* water.

I have learned through the years that diversity is an excellent thing in mentorship. If you seek counsel only from the same person for years and years, you will become a devoted disciple of your mentor, not of Christ. We see this all the time, specifically with celebrity preachers or writers. People have a tendency to follow what they say and write, and before long, they are just regurgitating their teachings. However, when you draw from many wells, your various mentors challenge you in different ways. You learn to appreciate them for different reasons. They even challenge you to carefully consider what other mentors have taught you, thus helping you be more assured of your beliefs and more able to defend them.

I have had mentors who were businessmen, professors, ministers, coaches, administrators, missionaries, and even a farmer or two. Their wealth of knowledge, drawn from experiences in many different fields, has added diversity and depth to my understanding. It also has helped me become a more well-rounded mentor since I draw frequently from what I learned from each of these other individuals when I mentor my apprentices.

Five Kinds of Mentors

It has been my experience that God sends different types of mentors into our lives at different times. They don't all look the same, and they certainly don't mentor in the same ways. As the needs of the apprentice change, so do the mentors God sends our way. Here are the five basic kinds of mentors I have had in my life and how they worked. You should be able to see this play out chronologically as you read through the letters.

Foundational Mentors

Foundational mentors establish you in who you are and what you believe. They found you in the fundamental things of your faith. They show you some of the character traits and basic practices of a new Christian such as reading your Bible, sharing your faith, understanding fundamental doctrines, and establishing some initial spiritual disciplines in your life.

A good example of a foundational mentor is Eli in 1 Samuel. When the boy Samuel was hearing from the Lord but did not recognize what was happening, Eli gave the boy these simple instructions: "If He [God] calls you, say, 'Speak, Lord, for your servant is listening'" (1 Sam. 3:9). That simple advice served Samuel all the years of his life.

Building Mentors

Building mentors help you determine your purpose and what to do with your future. These people introduce you to the rest of your life. As you move into the calling and task you have received, they help you learn the terrain and how to live and succeed in this new world. They build on the foundation that has already been laid and teach you the rules of the world. Having a calling and a purpose is part of being intentional with your spiritual growth. It indicates a deeper purpose but not necessarily a specific vocation.

Paul's relationship with young Timothy exemplifies this type of mentorship perfectly. Timothy's faith was first established by the efforts of his grandmother, Lois, then by his mother, Eunice. Paul built on the foundation that was so expertly laid by these women, helping Timothy understand his gifting as a teacher of God's Word and his calling to establish each church in sound doctrine.

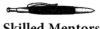

Skilled Mentors

Skilled mentors help you determine the necessary skills needed to fulfill your calling. They may help you with a specific ability such as teaching, leading, or mentoring—or even a practical skill such as carpentry or blacksmithing. They can mentor you life-on-life or even from afar, but they invest in your success because they want to pass on what they have learned to the next generation and see their work continue through you.

When Priscilla and Aquila first met Apollos, they recognized that although he knew scripture very well and was an eloquent man, his understanding of the gospel was lacking. So they took him to their home and explained the way of God to him more accurately. Apollos continued in ministry in Achaia and beyond, working alongside Paul for years. For that to have happened, he needed that time with Priscilla and Aquila. They gave him the very thing he needed to proclaim the gospel accurately.

Weathervane Mentors

Weathervane mentors help you read the world around you and recognize the signs as the winds change. You can have these at any time, but they are most common during the last stages of your mentorship journey. They focus on deep conversations about things you would not have understood earlier in your journey. As you see the signs of change, you may be able to interpret what God is doing around you so you can find your place in His plan.

Peter understood that the Gentiles played a mysterious part in God's plan and in establishing the kingdom of Jesus (Acts 11), but he got confused when he was with his Jewish friends. He wasn't entirely sure how things were shifting. However, Paul had seen Gentiles accept Jesus as Messiah and king, while most of his Jewish countrymen rejected Jesus and preferred the worship of their religious traditions. As odd as it seems, God used Paul and his travels and experiences to help Peter understand that he was deviating from the truth of the gospel. It took a Pharisee of Pharisees to explain to Peter the fullness of what God was doing. Peter humbly accepted the correction, and the future of his ministry reflects that paradigm shift.

Situational Mentors

Situational mentors are people you may not be walking with day to day. You don't sit down with them regularly to discuss life and how you are doing. However, you have watched them and have developed a deep respect for them and their walk with the Lord. So when you have to make big decisions or are going through a trial, you call on them to ask them to speak into the situation and give counsel.

The first church in Jerusalem was very Jewish, but the new wine of the Holy Spirit was breaking the wineskin of their traditions. Gentiles were coming to follow the Jewish Messiah. Was that allowed? Could it be that God was reaching beyond their perceptions? The elders in Jerusalem were not sure what to do with what was happening. So they chose a good man, the son of encouragement, who was full of the Holy Spirit and faith, to help them decipher the situation. His name was Barnabas, and he was called on to take a look into these Gentile believers, testify as to what he had seen and what the Holy Spirit had revealed to him, and give the Jewish church good counsel.

As we develop a culture of mentorship, we must learn to honor those who have poured into us and walked with us on the path, guiding us and helping us avoid pitfalls. In this book, I also would like to honor some of the men and women who have poured into me over the years and say a sincere thank you for not giving up on me and for taking time out of their busy lives to make me into who I am today.

I hope this book will help you consider those who have mentored you and how you can share your appreciation with them. However, above all, I deeply desire that this book will empower you to be a better apprentice and mentor so the truths that have been passed on to you will be rooted into the next generation as well.

Note: When you read the kind words, I'm not trying to puff myself up. I'm trying to demonstrate how important it is as a mentor to build up and encourage those you are mentoring.

CHAPTER 2
FOUNDATIONS

Show me a successful individual and I'll show you someone who had real positive influences in his or her life. I don't care what you do for a living—if you do it well, I'm sure there was someone cheering you on or showing the way. A mentor.

—Denzel Washington

Bill and Nadine Taliaferro
Faithfulness, Perseverance, and Hard Work

Context: The year is 1991. I am a freshman in high school. The last decade has been pretty tough on everyone. I got in a lot of trouble at school. I was unsure of myself, my heart was full of anger and bitterness, and I would run my mouth constantly. I was hateful to my parents and nearly everyone else who really loved me. Then I had a life-changing encounter with Jesus. Everything changed. My actions finally caught up with my knowledge. My parents had endured the rough years and loved me when I was literally unlovable. Now they were finally seeing the fruit of their unconditional love, patience, and faith play out in my life.

Dear Jeremy,

Son, your mother and I have been praying for you since before you were even born. There have been some rough patches, but as we see where God has brought you, we are very proud of the young man you are becoming. You have found your way, and His name is Jesus. We know from experience that following after Him is the best possible path, and it will allow you to develop into the man God wants you to be. As you grow and prepare to go into the world to make an impact for His kingdom, we want to share with you some important thoughts to help you to maintain proper focus.

Beware of money. The scripture says that the love of money is the root of all kinds of evil. We want to warn you that it can sneak in without even recognizing it. The best way to avoid falling into this trap is to learn early that the money and the resources you have do not belong to you. They belong to the Lord, and He has given them to you so you can further His kingdom, not your own. If you are faithful with your resources and a good steward, the Lord will make sure you have whatever is needed to fulfill the task He has given you. This doesn't mean you will always be rich, but if you learn to think of money in a proper way, you will never be poor. You will understand that when you are older.

Be faithful. Don't waver from what you know is true. Right is right, and wrong is wrong. Don't ever deceive yourself into doing what you know is wrong. Be faithful to your Lord, to your family, to your church, to your friends, and to your future wife. Be faithful to the calling you have received. The Lord wants you to be steady and trustworthy. That is what a good worker looks like, whether it is in ministry or a secular job.

We have tried to fulfill the Lord's purpose in our lives. We are not preachers or missionaries, but God made me a businessman and your mom a nurse. We have strived to serve the Lord through our work and the relationships that come with that. We all have a purpose in His kingdom. No purpose is greater or lesser than another because they all serve Him. Your mom and I have known your purpose since you were young. In fact, I distinctly remember dedicating you before the Lord, as Hannah did with Samuel, in our living room when you were just a baby. You have a gift. Use it for His glory, and never misuse your talents to build yourself up.

Do what He made you for. It may seem impossible at times, but I promise you that if you work hard and lean on Him, you can accomplish anything He sends you to do. I know He will give you some things that seem difficult to bear. Never give up! Keep pushing forward so He may be glorified in your life and people will come to know Jesus because of your faithfulness, perseverance, and hard work.

We love you, son!
Dad

Outcome of this letter on my life: After devoting my life to Christ during my freshman year of high school, I was blessed to have two people in my home who really walked the walk. They continue to inspire me and encourage me to this day. Not everyone gets to have one godly parent, but God sent me *two* because he knew I would need them. Their patience and perseverance during my troubled years was founded on their devotion to Christ, and they truly loved me like Jesus through those times. I still carry the shame of the hateful words I uttered to them in my most selfish and self-absorbed moments. But they were shining examples of unconditional love. They told the truth in love, never budged from what was right and wrong, and never wavered in their love and care for me—even when I didn't deserve it.

Mentoring strategies used:
- Modeling
- Wise counsel
- Confronting
- Correcting
- Teaching life skills

How we spent time together: For 18 years, I lived under my parents' roof. I saw who they really were, day in and day out. Their consistency and character had a lasting impact on my life.

How I reproduce the investment: With my own children, I model before I teach. I never ask someone to do something I haven't done. I teach by doing. I teach absolute truth, and I don't compromise for the sake of convenience.

> *Train up a child in the way he should go;*
> *even when he is old he will not depart from it.*
> —Prov. 22:6 ESV

FOUNDATIONS

Dr. Jack Dale
Stepping out of Your Comfort Zone

Context: It's 1992. I have left behind my old life, and I am striving to walk with the Lord. High school was full of temptation, and I was honestly full of myself and more than a little self-righteous. I was the guy who wore the Christian T-shirt, had a bunch of tracts in my back pocket, and told my friends their music was satanic. My love of the Lord was genuine; I was just lacking maturity and humility. Jack Dale was my youth minister, and he invited a few other guys and me over to his house regularly. His wife cooked for us, we played video games, and we played with his kids. Then Jack opened the scripture, and we were blown away by what he taught us. No question was off-limits. We talked about things that challenged our beliefs and our view of the world. It helped us see Jesus in a whole new light. Being a Christian wasn't as boring as we had thought. It opened up a whole new world for me.

> *Hey, bud,*
>
> *I'm so proud of you and stoked to see you fully sold out to the Lord. I promise I will be here for you as you take this journey of faith. I know as a young person, there are so many things pulling at you and vying for your attention. Be focused. Learn the difference between a distraction and a worthy endeavor. The best way to do that is by digging into God's Word. Man, I'm telling you it is so full of mysteries and wonder. It's like getting a glimpse of who God really is. There are things in the Bible I don't understand, but as I study, I learn more and more about who He is and about His character. That will change you from the inside, and those inside changes will manifest themselves in your behavior.*

Learn to love His Word; it is the source of all knowledge. Others will tell you differently, especially when you go to college, but if you always devote yourself to His Word, it will give you direction in your life and wisdom for walking the path He has laid out for you.

Be consistent in your faith. Dry spells are normal; don't worry. God has not left you. He is just allowing you to show that you will be faithful to what you have learned thus far. Don't be distracted by the desire for popularity, but love your friends with a holy love. Share the gospel with your friends who are lost, and give them an opportunity to know the peace you have found. Don't be embarrassed by the gospel. Be bold, and proclaim the truth with courage.

Sexual desires are normal and given to you by God, but you must learn to put your desires into submission to Christ. Protect yourself from sexual immorality; don't put yourself in impossible situations. Make open commitments to purity before others, and let them keep you accountable.

Step outside of your world! Things are safe and comfortable here in your hometown, but people outside are hurting, and He has given us the task of easing their suffering. It is scary at first, but if you step out there, you will find your true purpose in Christ. You are to be light in darkness. You should never be afraid of the darkness because you are in the light.

Serve the homeless, the poor, and the hungry. Reach out to the forgotten ones, and share the hope of Jesus with them. If they come to follow Jesus, it could change them, but I promise that it will change you as you live a life of obedience, even when it is uncomfortable.

FOUNDATIONS

> *One last thing: Live your life and have fun! No matter where you find yourself, if the life you are living in Christ is not full of joy and excitement, you are doing it wrong. Don't take yourself too seriously. Laugh and enjoy the freedom we have in Christ!*
>
> Jack Dale

Outcome of this letter on my life: During Jack's time at First Baptist Church of Springtown, at least four young men surrendered to the ministry. All four of us are serving the Lord in different capacities today. Much of that is due to the investment Jack made in us. We would not have recognized the need or even the voice of the Lord speaking in our lives if he had not taken the time to mentor a bunch of high schoolers. So you see, a small-town youth minister can have a massive impact all over the world by merely mentoring the people God sends his way.

Mentoring strategies used:
- Modeling
- Studying scripture together
- Challenging Christian norms
- Asking hard questions
- Requiring me to do hard things
- Accountability

How we spent time together: I spent a lot of time in Jack's home. We also spent time casually hanging out at his office in the church. It usually started casually and informally, such as playing video games in his living room or talking about our day, but we often seemed to find ourselves wrapped in deep conversation about scripture or the daily Christian life.

How I reproduce the investment: I welcome people I am mentoring into my home. We have meals together, watch movies, and live life together. That makes it easier to transition into the deeper things of life when the time is right, and it helps my apprentices see me as a real person instead of some spiritual guru or celebrity preacher.

I also like to push the boundaries of what is comfortable in ministry. I like for the people I am mentoring to experience the uneasiness of ministering to "the least of these" (Matt. 25:40). I want them to rub shoulders with people who are suffering and with those who are marginalized because it helps them gain perspective on what the world is really like outside of their Christian echo chamber.

> *We cared so much for you that we were pleased to share with you not only the gospel of God but also our own lives, because you had become dear to us.*
> —1 Thess. 2:8

CHAPTER 3
PREPARATION

Do not train a child to learn by force or harshness; but direct them to it by what amuses their minds, so that you may be better able to discover with accuracy the peculiar bent of the genius of each.

—Plato

Jeff Glenn
Finding Identity

Context: It is 1996. I am in college at Hardin-Simmons University. My walk with the Lord is growing, and I am finding some maturity as people pour into me and I come to know, understand, and obey the Word of God. Jeff Glenn was my small-group leader in a youth function in 1990 when he confronted my double life in a bold but gentle way. He challenged me to choose whom I would serve. I did.

Years later, after my freshman year in college, Jeff invited me to come and pour into his students as a youth intern at the First Baptist Church in Cairo, Georgia. It was a challenging time but one where I grew tremendously as I learned to die to self and serve with my whole heart. Much of what I learned was because of direct mentorship from Jeff and his wife, Malea.

> *Hey, J,*
>
> *As I remember back to when we first met, things were very different then. You were living a double life, even as a teenager. You went to church and claimed to be a follower, but your life did not demonstrate devotion to the Lord. But now it's like night and day. I remember confronting you and encouraging you to decide who you would follow. To see you follow 100 percent after the Lord has really blessed me. No matter what happens, stay the course. Fully devote yourself to Him and give Him your life. You will not regret it.*
>
> *Don't be drawn into the desire to find your identity in something other than who you are in Christ. Believe me, you will be fulfilled if you learn to be His obedient*

son. It's okay to look and dress differently. Be who you are, man! God made you different for His own purposes. I don't mind the tattoos and the mohawk; in fact, I love being around you because you are so willing to be wildly different. But if you find your identity in those things, in that image, you will be disappointed, and it will ultimately lead you to idolatry.

Don't try to be a superstar or seek fame. Be faithful to the specific task that God calls you to do, even if it isn't glamorous. It is better to be faithful to God and considered an obedient servant than to seek fame in this world and use what God gave you to build your kingdom instead of His.

Find a godly woman to partner with you in life and ministry. She will sometimes be the only one who supports and believes in you as God leads you both into strange and sometimes dangerous places. She will challenge you and support you in ways no one else can. But don't go seeking her out; let God bring her to you in the right timing.

I love you, my younger brother, and I look forward to many years of co-laboring together!

Jeff Glenn

Outcome of this letter on my life: Jeff and his wife, Malea, are some of the most gentle and loving people I have ever known. But strangely enough, God used them to say very confrontational things to me at a time when I really needed it. They taught with words, but mostly their actions challenged me and helped me see some of the issues in my own heart. I really appreciate their example and how they held me to a higher standard. I also learned so much from seeing them serve side by side as a team for all those years. It helped me tremendously to know what a healthy marriage should look like in the context of ministry.

Mentoring strategies used:
- Generously giving time and resources
- Recommending and discussing books
- Providing accountability
- Modeling maturity

How we spent time together: My time with Jeff has always come in bursts. I would get a week to a couple months with Jeff, and then we wouldn't see each other for a year or more. But when we were together, we spent most of our time in his home or office. Once again, our time was informal, but usually it was focused on spiritual growth and what God was doing in my life at that time.

How I reproduce the investment: I challenge young men and women to surrender fully to the purposes God has for their lives and to hold nothing back from Him. There is no room for mediocrity. Either your life is about Christ or it is about you. I help young men see through the cultural mandates that are pressing in on them and find their true identity in Christ. It is so easy to avoid difficult conversations with people you are mentoring, but I love my apprentices enough to confront the issues that are hindering them from growth.

> *Every branch in Me that does not produce fruit He removes, and He prunes every branch that produces fruit so that it will produce more fruit.*
> —John 15:2

PREPARATION

Jesse Fletcher
Man's Greatest Endeavor

Context: It is 1998 at Hardin-Simmons University. My faith has grown, and I feel strongly that God has called me to the mission field. I have been mentored by professors, church leaders, older Christians, and school administrators. I have devoted myself to studying and proclaiming God's Word. I have become active in serving at the Salvation Army shelter. I have begun preparing for the mission field by reading many missionary biographies and studying missiology. My university career is coming to a close, and I have to decide what I will do next. I know I want to go overseas to serve, but with what organization? Those decisions will forever impact my life. Dr. Jesse Fletcher was a strong dose of wisdom and experience during a pivotal time in my life.

Dear Jeremy,

As you prepare to go to the mission field, I want to share some insights with you that might help you along the path. The missionary life is adventurous and exciting in many ways, but it also is infinitely difficult. If you go into this calling unprepared, you will find much trouble, both physical and spiritual. It is imperative that you prepare yourself beforehand as much as possible for the situations you may encounter. Think about the possible outcomes or difficulties and prepare for those contingencies ahead of time. Then, when you are in a stressful situation, you will already know what to do.

What will you say when you are asked to preach the first time you visit a church? Be prepared.

What will you do when sexual temptation comes knocking on your door? Be prepared.

What will you do when disaster strikes? Be prepared.

The missionary life is not all roses. Sometimes you have to make hard decisions and things don't go as planned. But if you find yourself standing on the Rock—the firm foundation of Jesus Christ—you will not be shaken.

I know you hate to be like everyone else. You are a nonconformist, and that is okay to a point. We need people who color outside the lines, who see things from a different perspective. Those people are infinitely important, especially in the missions world. We need creative strategies to get the gospel to some of the most difficult places in the world. But when your nonconformity makes you less effective for the kingdom, it is not beneficial, and it doesn't help you or Christ's church. I know you have trouble trusting some organizations. It is part of how your generation questions things, but ask yourself this: Will I be more effective for His kingdom with or without the organization? It may make you feel good to buck the system. It may gain you prestige with your peers. But if it harms or slows down the advance of Christ's kingdom, is it really worth it? You must learn to work with even those you don't agree with 100 percent and make godly compromises. That is part of dying to yourself and putting His endeavors above your own.

Use your creativity to extend His kingdom into unreached areas. Build God's kingdom, not your own. Devote your whole life to His service; it is a person's greatest endeavor.

Jesse Fletcher

Outcome of this letter on my life: Dr. Fletcher was the first one to give me a glimpse into the real life of a missionary. He was so cutting-edge in his teaching style, and it made the world of cross-cultural ministry come alive to me. I realized that every decision I made had implications. He prepared me for looking at the big picture, developing a strategy, and implementing it, but he also taught me to be flexible enough to change when circumstances changed. I just had a short couple of years with Dr. Fletcher. I wish it could have been more. But in the little time I did have with him, God used him to prepare me for the future He had in store for me. I would say that 80 percent of the decisions I make day to day are influenced by Dr. Fletcher. Everyone should have someone like him in their lives.

Mentoring strategies used:
- Classroom lectures
- Asking hard questions
- Case studies
- Debriefing decisions and ideas
- Telling pertinent stories from his life

How we spent time together: My time with Dr. Fletcher was usually in his classroom or office where we would develop strategies and debrief outcomes. He brought real-life experience into his classroom, and we always felt he was preparing us for the actual problems we would encounter on the mission field. It was not just theory, so we soaked up every word he said.

How I reproduce the investment: For many years, I have trained new missionaries in the same style Dr. Fletcher trained me. We deal with real issues and problems, and we debrief, debrief, and then debrief again. Just like Dr. Fletcher, I train my apprentices to think through their answers to the hard questions and situations before they happen so they are guided by logic, research, and scriptural models, not swayed by emotion or fear.

> *Plans fail when there is no counsel, but with many advisers they succeed.*
>
> —Prov. 15:22

James Shields
Serious-Mindedness

Context: It's 1998. I am one of many theology students at Hardin-Simmons University. Many of the professors and administrators are quite distinguished—former missionaries, Greek and Hebrew scholars, theological geniuses, and so on. But there is only one "gray fox"—Dr. James Shields. He looked like a mix between an old country preacher and a drill sergeant. And frankly, that may have been exactly what he was. Everyone was intimidated by him, and he had a reputation of telling it exactly like it was. I was terrified of his class. I had long hair and tattoos and did not fit the typical mold of a West Texas preacher. For two semesters, I thought he was going to terrorize me. To my surprise, my appearance never came up. Dr. Shields focused on character and devotion to the Word. I had been preaching since I was 14, but this was a whole new world for me. Today, I don't preach exactly in the style that Dr. Shields taught, but to this day, I still live and teach many things he taught me about character and a devoted study of the Word.

> Jeremy,
>
> *The ministry of the Word is a very serious matter. There is great responsibility in proclamation. You must learn to bring serious-mindedness to the task. A man of God should prepare to share a message with study and devoted time with one's Creator, not looking for jokes and silly illustrations. If that is all you have to offer, don't bother to undertake this task.*
>
> *Study of the Word should be your life. Dig deep to try to understand the meaning so you are true to the text as*

you preach. Exegete passages to learn the intended meaning and avoid eisegesis (reading your own beliefs into the text). The Bible should be your foundation. It informs our behaviors and beliefs, which should never influence how you interpret scripture. That's getting it backward.

Your voice and presence are tools given to you by God; care for them well. Presentation is a skill you should study and refine. Rid your preaching of anything that would distract from the message of God's Word. If you have mindless gestures, control them so they don't distract from His message. If you have humor, use it carefully, only to help people connect with the text, not for people to like you. In all things, use self-control, and submit to the Lord the gifts He has given you.

Don't think too highly of yourself, and never let pride take root in your life. It will be the end of your effectiveness in ministry. Be humble in word and deed.

Proclamation is a great privilege, but real ministry is done outside of those tasks. It happens at 2:00 a.m. when someone needs you to help them walk through a trial. Or it may happen when you have to set aside something you enjoy to serve someone in a way that will bring no glory to yourself. In most cases, if it is convenient for you, it really isn't ministry. Real ministry is never convenient.

I hope these insights will help you as you follow the direction God is leading you in.

Dr. James Shields

Outcome of this letter on my life: I would not be writing this book if it had not been for Dr. Shields. He taught me how to study God's Word like a scholar and how to organize my thoughts in a way that would communicate truth. I was nervous at first to even enter his class, but he treated me with respect and honor. He became one of my heroes of the faith. I use his life as an example to those I teach and disciple on a regular basis. He is a true example of a good tree that bore much fruit.

Mentoring strategies used:
- Classroom lecture
- Modeling
- Critiquing and debriefing performance
- Asking about motives

How we spent time together: For two years, I spent time in the classroom of the man we called the Gray Fox. That is where I learned the skills he imparted. But for decades after leaving Hardin-Simmons University, I have watched Dr. Shields's life from a distance. I feel strongly about this man because of what I saw outside the classroom, not because of what I heard in the classroom.

How I reproduce the investment: I study and research everything I teach. I train my apprentices to know the scripture and dedicate themselves to its study. When I teach Bible storying techniques, I use a critique process very similar to Dr. Shields's, which forces students to be aware of how well they are keeping with the text and how their presentation helps or hurts the understanding and retention of the Bible story.

> *A wise man's instruction is a fountain of life,*
> *turning people away from the snares of death.*
> —Prov. 13:14

PREPARATION

Linda Carleton
Learning to Listen

Context: It is the late 1990s. I'm still at Hardin-Simmons University. I was the epitome of a big fish from a little pond learning to adjust to being a little fish in a big pond. University life was a big shift for me. The student body of my university had more people than my hometown. The university was also very diverse culturally, which was new for me. I really wasn't the student government type, and I may have been called to the dean's office on a couple of occasions for dumb shenanigans. But somewhere along the way, the dean, Linda Carleton, took an interest in me and began to give me opportunities to grow outside of my comfort zone—exposing me to other perspectives. Through her, I learned what leadership should look like.

Jeremy,

Thank you for your leadership over the past couple of years. It has been encouraging to see you develop and grow as a leader. I look forward to seeing how you grow in the years to come. Remember, almost anyone can be a leader, but it takes something different to demonstrate leadership. Some people have a commanding presence or a charisma that draws people to them; they are in their very nature leaders. But to demonstrate leadership, one must be disciplined and focused. You must be measured in your responses and learn to thrive in diverse environments.

Surround yourself with friends from diverse backgrounds, find common ground, and work together to accomplish something important. I know you came from a small town where there wasn't much opportunity to learn about other cultures and perspectives, but since you have been here, you have earned the respect of people from all backgrounds. That is the beginning of demonstrating leadership. Everyone isn't going to like you or agree with you, but be respectful and learn to listen—really listen—not just being quiet while waiting for your turn to argue your perspective. Listen, try to understand why they feel like they do, and put yourself in their shoes.

Seek unity in diversity. It is a very difficult but worthwhile goal. Most people who have experienced unity have only seen it in a mostly homogenous environment. But unity with diversity is rare and very powerful. If it can be maintained, people will stand up and take notice.

Put your efforts toward something worthwhile. Don't waste your energies on endeavors that are too small or don't have a lasting impact. Now get out there and change the world!

Linda Carleton

Outcome of this letter on my life: Linda Carleton had strong beliefs but wasn't threatened by beliefs that differed from hers. She truly listened. When I was talking, I knew she wasn't only listening but also trying to understand my perspective. This has been one of the most beneficial things I have ever been taught. As a missionary, it is very important for me to think about the people I serve and understand where they are coming from. That allows me to meet their needs and speak to the core of who they are. It has helped me be a better communicator, as well as a better leader.

PREPARATION

Mentoring strategies used:
- Modeling
- Small-group discussions
- Research projects with presentations
- Informal conversations

How we spent time together: From time to time, I was with Linda Carleton in her office, discussing things I was learning. The majority of our time together, however, was in our unity group, a gathering of diverse students from different ethnic backgrounds who were brought together to talk about differences and find points of unity and agreement. She usually led these groups and asked questions that generated discussion and helped us understand different perspectives.

How I reproduce the investment: Multiethnic missionary teams have been a passion of mine. Integrating national partners into a mostly Western team is difficult but extremely productive. I love helping my apprentices learn to work alongside people of different cultures, ethnic backgrounds, and languages. It is a great way to stretch your team and help them grow in understanding and interpersonal skills.

> *How good and pleasant it is when God's people live together in unity!*
>
> —Ps. 133:1 NIV

CHAPTER 4
TO THE NATIONS

In order to be a mentor, and an effective one, one must care. You must care. You don't have to know how many square miles are in Idaho, you don't need to know what is the chemical makeup of chemistry, or of blood or water. Know what you know and care about the person.

—Maya Angelou

After I graduated from Hardin-Simmons University, I signed up to be a two-year Journeyman missionary in Peru through the International Mission Board. I would be working with an indigenous tribe called the Ashéninka, and I would be joining a team that already had been deployed and were just starting the work. The Ashéninka live in a very remote part of the Peruvian jungle where many rivers flow to form the headwaters of the Amazon River.

Chris Ammons
Love the Church

Context: When I arrived in Peru to work with the Ashéninka people in 1999, I was greeted by Chris Ammons in the most stiflingly hot, humid airport you can imagine. Within the first week, I knew I had been given a special opportunity to sit under a visionary. God had picked this assignment and this mentor just for me. It was the most difficult thing I had ever done, but Christ walked me through each step. He challenged my ideas, caused me to adjust my beliefs and practices, and gave me responsibility beyond my ability. That led me to exponential growth as I learned to lean on the Lord in ways I had never done before. And I had a spiritual father to help me process what I was learning. I was in my 20s, living with an Amazonian tribe and being mentored by a mighty man of God. That is what I had been planning and praying for most of my life.

J,

When you arrived, you told me you were planning on being a missionary the rest of your life and wanted me to teach you all I could. I have endeavored to do just that, and I would only ask that you do the same to those you train and teach in the years to come.

Wherever you find yourself, remember that although strategy is important, if you lose your passion for the lost, your work will become meaningless. Focus your efforts on the nations, set your sights on those who are forgotten and have not yet had the opportunity to hear the life-changing message of the gospel. Do whatever it takes to bring them the good news of Jesus.

If you must learn a language, then get to studying. If you have to change your proclamation style to fit their learning preference, do what is best for them, not what is comfortable for you. Whatever it takes to get the gospel to the lost, that is what we are called to do. Clearly, God has called you to this task. Do not be diverted from this holy calling by anyone or anything.

And don't just stop with the gospel of salvation. That is just the first step. Once they have come into the fold, give them the church—the ekklesia—the assembly of believers. It is through the magnificent body of Christ that they will come to know and understand who they are in Christ.

But first, you must fully understand the Bride, learn about the church, know what it is supposed to do, and discover how God's people should live and function within the body. Believe me, it is much bigger than what you have known. The church is more than buildings and Sunday meetings. It is the secret to abundant life and spiritual growth. It is the solution to the world's problems.

Focus your life and teachings on the church. Do not separate the message of salvation through Jesus from the church. The head and the body together, that is the full message of hope. As you come to understand the church, you will find your place and your calling. Serve Jesus, and serve His church.

You are young and inexperienced, but don't let anyone diminish your passion. You are capable of doing great things if you surrender yourself to God and let Him work through you. He doesn't need you, but He will use you if your heart remains devoted to Him.

But beware! Things won't always come easily. You will be opposed, lied about, and held back. Organizations need visionaries, but they also hate them. Grow thick skin. It will get ugly. But learn to work within the system when you can. Apply appropriate pressure when you know your vision comes from God. Fight for what you believe in, but know you will make enemies with those who love the status quo. Above all, please God, not people.

Chris Ammons

Outcome of this letter on my life: Two years serving under Chris opened my eyes and my ministry to a more apostolic, big-picture understanding of the Great Commission. Chris gave me books to read, invited me into his home, and spoke with me on long car rides. All that allowed God to form me into the missionary He had called me to be. Chris treated me like a full-fledged missionary, not some short-term guy who needed his hand held. That helped me grow quickly into maturity in ministry because I was allowed to try, fail, debrief, and try again. All told, I served under Chris for almost four years. He and his wife, Pam, informed my missiology with a healthy dose of reality and vision. I am eternally grateful.

Mentoring strategies used:
- Debriefing decisions and ideas
- Modeling
- Challenging
- Giving responsibilities
- Recommending and discussing books
- Teaching

How we spent time together: My most productive times with Chris were in a truck, driving from place to place. We would talk about what we were going to do, do it, and then spend the trip back debriefing what we did and talking about how we could do it better the next time.

We spent time around the campfire at night talking about life and ministry and telling stories and jokes. I ate many meals in his home. We went out to eat together. I was basically his adopted son and spent every possible hour with him so I could learn what he knew.

How I reproduce the investment: I make time for single men and women who are eager but green. I make the most of travel time and debrief at every given opportunity. I major in ecclesiology. I love talking about the church and its place in the world. I love revealing the mysteries of the church and helping people find their rightful place in their local body and the world. I do it with a passion that I got from Chris.

> *Do what you have learned and received and heard and seen in me, and the God of peace will be with you.*
> —Phil. 4:9

Avery Willis
Prepare for a Helpmate

Context: I had been living in the jungle with the Ashéninkas for about a year. God had broken me of my pride and taught me a lot about obedience and trusting His Spirit to use me when I was incapable of the task. We saw many come to faith and maybe half a dozen churches planted. God was on the move, and I had the privilege of a front-row seat. The experience of watching Him transform people and even cultures was life-changing for me, and I still walk in the knowledge and understanding gained from that time. I was told by my boss Chris Ammons that one of the big shots from the International Mission Board (IMB) was coming for a visit, and they would be bringing him out to visit me in the village and see the work. I wasn't excited about it. I'm a little rough around the edges, and I'm not really good with the "suits." But Chris would not heed my warning. I'm so glad he didn't. Avery Willis was the furthest thing from a "suit" that there ever was. He was kind and humble and full of wisdom. In one week, he had a lasting impact on my life. I will never forget that time with this humble servant.

> *Dear J,*
>
> *I enjoyed my visit to see you and have been eternally impacted by what I saw God doing in the jungle there.*
>
> *Know that I will continue to pray for God to bring you a helpmate to join you in your work. A godly wife in this work is very important. In fact, I would even say it is eternally important because as she joins you and you work together in ministry, you will have an eternal impact on every soul you meet.*

I know your life as a single man has been good, and you seem to quite enjoy the freedom it offers you. It is true that you should take every advantage of those single years, but don't hide yourself from the next phase of life because, I promise you, it is equally rich.

Yes, as a single man you can often go harder and longer. You can stay out in a jungle village for months on end and test your physical limits. But as a married man, you can have a wider impact. You can minister to both men and women. You can impact the trajectory of families as they come to know and understand the gospel through the ministry of you and your wife.

As a father, you also can help other dads lead their families in the way of truth. You may even have the privilege of seeing the first generation of Christians among these tribes who will be teaching their children the gospel from their childhood—the beginnings of a heritage of faith.

So enjoy this stage of life, but know that God has a lot of goodness in the next stage as well.

As the time comes and you begin seeking a spouse, don't rely on your flesh or even logic to determine who you should marry. Wait on the Lord, and let Him bring the right helpmate to you. He is the only one who knows what your story will entail. He knows the trials you will face. He knows the places He will lead you. He knows what you will need through the various stages of your growth as a man.

Trust His leading, for He is the giver of all good things. He provided for Adam, and He will provide for you. When God makes it clear who your future wife is, be bold and courageous, and start right by leading her with humility and godliness.

I have no doubt that you will be mentoring young people and families as your ministry grows. Learn to lead with humility.

Mentor quietly, offer your help, but be humble. No matter how "successful" you become in ministry, keep yourself from pride.

Always listen and be open to learn new things, even from new missionaries. Know when to give counsel and when to listen and observe. Unsolicited advice is rarely heeded. So be careful with your words, and when someone seeks your counsel, make the very most of every word.

Avery Willis

Outcome of this letter on my life: Avery was one of the most humble men I have ever met, yet he was a wellspring of knowledge and wisdom. He was a devoted disciple, and it seemed so effortless for him, though I know it actually was born out of decades of obedient devotion to Christ.

In casual conversation, he was throwing out pearls of wisdom. I tried to pick up every single one of them. He specifically admonished me to find a helpmate to come alongside me in the task. He prayed for me multiple times in that jungle hut. He prayed that I would be prepared, and he prayed specifically for the woman God would bring to me. (Lord knows she would need all those prayers!)

Soon enough, God brought that special woman into my life, but not for long. Her name was Susan Fino. We had met initially when we were both going to the mission field with Journeymen. She went to Israel, and I went to Peru.

After completing our assignments, we got married. While we were in the process of returning to the field a few years later, I stopped by Avery's office in Richmond to introduce him to the woman he had prayed for. To my surprise, he remembered me and prayed with us for our future ministry together. It's a very special memory for us.

Mentoring strategies used:
- Active listening
- Words of wisdom
- Modeling

How we spent time together: We only spent one week together, but that week had a lasting impact on me. Avery sat with me and others around the evening fire, telling us stories and wisdom from his experiences. We talked from inside our mosquito nets before we went to sleep. We laughed as we bathed in the dirty river in the afternoons. It was all casual and fun. But he pulled me aside privately when he felt he had a specific and personal thing to share, and he prayed for me a very specific prayer. I knew that he cared for me personally, like a younger brother. I wasn't just one of the crowd to him. His personable nature really opened my heart to anything he might say.

How I reproduce the investment: I discuss the possibility of marriage with the singles I mentor. (It turns out Avery was totally right about that.) I raise my children with purpose and invest in them because I know that what they experience as missionary kids and what they see in our marriage will deeply affect their views of the world and their place in it.

Though I am not there yet, I am learning to model control of my tongue, making every word valuable and not speaking without purpose.

> *Imitate me, as I also imitate Christ.*
> —1 Cor. 11:1

Steve King
Mobilized to the Nations

Context: I got married in 2002 and returned to the field in 2003. Due to the great successes we saw among the Ashéninka people, we expanded our scope and started a new team called the Xtreme Team. Its mission was to take the gospel to all the tribes in our region that had not yet heard the gospel. We began to work in Peru, Bolivia, Ecuador, and Brazil. My mentor Chris Ammons had moved on to a new field of service, and I had replaced him as team leader. Honestly, I was in way over my head. I studied for hours every day. I prayed and begged the Lord to give me what I needed to fulfill the task He had given me. He did just that! One of the answers to that prayer was Steve King. He was our regional leader, an experienced missionary who helped me grow in my weaknesses and adapt my leadership style to fit a much larger task.

J,

As these new responsibilities have been put on your plate, let me give some guidance that will serve you as you grow into this new role.

Study God's Word and have a map and a list of unreached people groups nearby. You should always know the status of lostness in any area you live. Where are the lost people, why are they lost, what do they believe, how can we get them access to the gospel, and so on? Then mobilize your efforts and make it happen. Expand your vision to the nations. Ask God to give you the nations and then develop plans to reach them.

Read! Read! Read! Learn from those who went before you. How did they accomplish the task given them? What did God do through their obedience? What can you learn from their experiences? You have access to many very skilled missionaries at your fingertips. Take advantage of that and become the best you can be.

It seems God will be blessing you with many young men and women to work alongside you. Develop those relationships because they are the missionaries you will be working alongside in the future.

Remember how Chris invested in you as a young missionary? Now it is your turn to do the same. Take this opportunity to deeply disciple them and help them consider their walk with the Lord. The kingdom needs more serious young men to take the gospel to the nations.

J, you will always be an outside-the-box kind of guy, and I love that about you. That is what makes you effective. But you also must learn to work with the people in the box or you will rarely get anything done. They are the gatekeepers, and if they don't understand you and your motivations, they will never release you to do what God uniquely gifted you to do.

I have tried really hard to be a flexible leader, empowering you in your strengths but also encouraging you to develop your weaknesses. But when you lead, be sure to bend a little bit in the direction of their weaknesses. Help them overcome their challenges; don't just demand that they do so. Stay strong in the Lord, and do what you do best. Go to the ugliest and darkest places, and shine His light there.

Steve King

Outcome of this letter on my life: I served under Steve King in one form or another for my entire 10 years in South America. To this day, he still is a trusted friend and mentor. I read his posts on social media almost every day, and he is still pouring into me from afar.

During those 10 years in South America, God accomplished a lot for His kingdom. People heard the gospel, many were baptized, leaders were trained, and churches were planted. But most of all, God grew His kingdom in my heart, and much of that was due to Steve's steady prodding. And I know Steve could not have done it if not for Paula, the helpmate God sent him. She is the sweetest lady you will ever meet, and I think it somehow rubbed off on Steve.

Mentoring strategies used:
- Modeling
- Teaching life skills
- Debriefing decisions and ideas
- Active listening
- Accountability

How we spent time together: One thing I remember about my time with Steve is that when we were in a meeting, he was taking notes on the discussion. In later conversations, he revisited things I had said or committed to. He kept me accountable for the things I said.

I also remember many hours hovering over maps and numbers, talking about languages, and developing new strategies for taking the gospel to those who hadn't heard. Steve helped me take things more seriously and be well versed on the realities of lostness in the world around me. I learned it wasn't enough to give an inspirational speech. I needed to have the facts to back up my words.

How I reproduce the investment: Much of my personal library came by recommendation of Steve King. I lend those books freely and challenge people to think about their strategies and research before they make plans. I hold people accountable for their big ideas. And my first task in any new project or assignment is research and learning before developing a strategy.

> *For by wise guidance you can wage your war, and in abundance of counselors there is victory.*
> —Prov. 24:6 ESV

Randy Griffin
Capable and Humble

Context: In 2005, I took over the leadership of the Xtreme Team since Chris and Pam Ammons were called to serve in another area. I was now responsible for training, leading, and mentoring a very large team in some of the most difficult places in the world. I felt I was too young and ill-equipped for the task. I was looking for help. Chris, my mentor for more than five years, had left, and I needed someone to help me proceed with wisdom and vision. I thought of Randy Griffin.

I had first met Randy when I was serving with the Ashéninka people. He had come to volunteer with our team. Randy was different than anyone I had ever met and didn't fit any mold or stereotype. He was a firefighter, a man's man, skilled as a mentor with decades of experience, yet he had a very soft and kind heart. After watching Randy lead, I realized this task required me to take on a leadership style very similar to his. I reached out to him so many times during those years, and he gave rich counsel. He would come out to serve, and I would soak up all the wisdom he provided. He was (and still is) a godsend.

> Hey, J,
>
> I'm guessing with Chris and Pam leaving it has left you feeling a bit overwhelmed, and I totally understand that. You have a lot of new stuff on your plate.
>
> So let me give you a little advice. Don't focus too much on your job and the responsibilities that seem overwhelming. Do your job well and work hard, but don't be defined by your job. That will lead to dissatisfaction.

TO THE NATIONS

It is much better to be defined by your walk with Christ and by the lives of the men and women you influence. That is your true fruit. Let their lives be your legacy. Build deep bonds with those young men and women, live life together, laugh together, and help them walk through their struggles as they help you walk through yours.

Don't be afraid to be vulnerable in front of them. They will respect you for the transparency. If you build a good team, a family, a band of brothers, they will walk with you into the deepest darkest parts of the world to serve our great King and Savior, Jesus Christ. They won't hesitate to suffer with you if you earn their respect, and you will be built up together because of enduring these trials.

Never stop learning new things. The whole world is out there with new experiences and challenges for us to conquer and master. Seek new challenges every day, and life will never be boring.

Become accomplished in the things that make you a man. Learn to be at home in the wilderness, help people in need, protect those who cannot protect themselves, and lead people into a deep relationship with Jesus. That is what it means to be a man. That is the core of who He created us to be. Live with these concepts at the core of who you are, and you will be content and fulfilled.

I know you are just coming into fatherhood and don't yet understand completely what that means and what it requires of you. But God has given you the responsibility of these young people at this time. During their time with you, they will need a fatherly example and role model.

When you don't know what to do, think of your own father and how he led you. Also think of how Jesus led His disciples and how Paul led with his co-laborers.

Give them wise counsel, but let them do.

Give them direction, but then let them go.

Do not micromanage or control, or they will never grow.

Give seemingly impossible tasks to the people you lead, and then debrief them. Whether they did well or encountered failure, help them think through how they can grow and make the best of even their failures.

When you are not sure what to do:
Debrief.
Talk through it.
And see what God reveals.

Brother, these young men and women are looking for someone to look up to. Live in such a way so you earn that right, but never become proud or impressed by your own abilities or accomplishments.

The thing that brings this all together is humility. Remember that everything good you have to give and everything you have accomplished ultimately did not come from you. It was a gift from God and was provided by Him. If you remember that, pride can't creep in.

I love you, brother,
Randy Griffin

P.S. Don't forget how to practice your knots!

Outcome of this letter on my life: Randy is one of my favorite people in the world. I truly do not think I would have made it through some of my roughest years without his support. He is one of the most sacrificial and loving men you will ever meet. Here's what always struck me about Randy: He is the most capable person you will ever encounter. He literally can do everything (and do it better than anyone else)—including kayaking and cycling, engine repair and medical "repair" (he has patched me up so many times), serving and leading. He excels at everything. But when you are with him, you just feel good about who you are, and you think you can do anything, too. He instilled in me a healthy, Christlike confidence and drive that allowed us to accomplish near-impossible tasks. I am not sure he has ever understood how widespread his impact really was and is. I am so grateful for such a faithful friend.

Mentoring strategies used:
- Debriefing decisions and ideas
- Teaching life skills
- Active listening
- Modeling
- Coaching
- Reassurance
- Encouragement

How we spent time together: In the early years, we spent time in dugout canoes, treating people for medical conditions, training young men together in the jungle, even getting homemade tattoos on remote Amazonian beaches. No topic was off-limits. We both were open books and lived like older and younger brothers.

We don't see each other as much these days, so when I need Randy or his counsel, I call him and catch up over the phone. He tells me of his victories and struggles, and I do the same. I always hang up the phone encouraged and ready to take on the task at hand.

How I reproduce the investment: I debrief everything. I find it helpful to talk frankly about our defeats as well as our victories.

When I find an occasion to recognize someone's hard work, I do it in front of their peers. It feels good to be recognized and appreciated.

I give people I mentor tasks that seem just beyond the reach of what they think they can do. How they respond to the challenge tells me a lot about their character. How they respond when they fail or succeed tells me even more.

I have learned that being painfully transparent builds deep bonds with people. Apprentices need to know that their mentor isn't perfect. It gives them hope.

Iron sharpens iron, and one man sharpens another.
—Prov. 27:17

TO THE NATIONS

Jerry Rankin
Protect Your Flock

Context: It's 2007. Leading the Xtreme Team involves a lot of moving parts. We had missionaries in four countries working with remote peoples in the Amazon jungle and the Andes. Some of those missionaries with our organization were from the United States. Others were national brothers and sisters sent out by their local churches and financially supported by those congregations.

It was really awesome to be part of a multicultural team with North Americans, Peruvians, Bolivians, Chileans, Ecuadorians, Colombians, Argentinians, Brazilians, and even Texans. Our team at the time got a lot of press in the missions world, and we got a lot of support and encouragement from our organization and supporting churches.

But not everyone was keen on what we did. There was one incident in Bolivia when a volunteer on a short-term trip encountered some of our national brothers on their way out to minister in a remote tribe. That individual did not like the fact that our organizations did not pay these national partners (though they were financially supported by their home churches), and he didn't like the idea that we were focusing on church planting and not evangelism and discipleship (though one cannot happen without the other).

He decided to raise a stink and make wild accusations about our team and my leadership, even though he had never met me. He put words into the mouths of our national brothers and used them to further his own agenda within our denomination. I had no idea any of this was going on as most of it was happening in the United States and was well above my pay grade.

But my boss at the time called and asked me a few questions to confirm and then a few weeks later explained to me what had been happening. This man had written a letter to Jerry Rankin, the president of our organization, making accusations and threatening statements. I knew Dr. Rankin. We had met on multiple occasions, and he was very supportive of what we were doing—even once taking a trip into the Amazon.

When Dr. Rankin received the letter, he responded by writing a letter of his own, defending us and our strategy and, frankly, our reputations. Steve King sent me a copy of the letter, which illustrates how good leaders stick their necks out for their people. Though most people focused primarily on Dr. Rankin's organizational leadership, it was his personal leadership that taught me the most.

> *Dear Jeremy,*
>
> *I am sorry you had to experience that unfortunate side of the missions world. Sometimes, people look only for trouble and opportunities to extend their own kingdoms. They are so consumed with their own agendas that they miss the miraculous things God is doing right in front of them.*
>
> *But I want to encourage you in this. You are out there on the edge; you see the world from a different vantage point. In most of these areas, the status quo will not accomplish the task. We must innovate, develop new strategies, and look to make the most of the situation we find ourselves in.*
>
> *So seek the Lord, and don't be afraid to dream big. Sometimes, He will lead you to do something out of the box, something that has never been done. That is a hard road to walk because people will oppose you. And sometimes, it is the people you would least expect.*
>
> *But God's plans are bigger than the small people who would oppose them. Be sure that what you want to do comes from the Lord. And once you are sure, hold fast to it and be obedient to the calling He has given you. He has His purposes for the direction He has given you. Trust Him and obey.*

Grow thick skin, and be willing to endure gossip and lies, but live in such a way that those who lie about you will be put to shame.

Another thing: Protect your people from the wolves who would discourage and distract them. Never let anyone speak poorly in your presence of someone you lead. Stand up for them with boldness and protect their reputation.

You know that everyone you lead still has areas in which they need to grow. All of us do. But don't allow others to tear down your people or exaggerate their flaws. If you have their backs and support them in this way, they will follow you into the most difficult places in the world and go into battle with you. They will face the enemy with courage at your side because they trust you and have been convinced of your brotherly love.

These are the bonds that lesser people long for but rarely see because it requires self-sacrifice and devotion to one another.

Spiritual warfare is a very real thing, and until we begin to see life through the lens of spiritual war, we will continue to fail both in our personal lives and in the Great Commission. So prepare yourself, build your team, and take the gospel into enemy territory.

Jerry Rankin

Outcome of this letter on my life: Rankin was a controversial figure in Baptist life, but I never really paid much attention to the politics. I was more concerned with learning from the man. I never spent long periods of time with him, but I learned to admire many of his character traits and tried to implement them in my own leadership. I have strived to be fiercely loyal to those I lead, and I have come to expect that from my leaders as well. That character trait has gotten me in trouble a couple of times (as I'm sure it did Dr. Rankin as well), but I wouldn't change it for the world.

I saw Dr. Rankin in 2016 at the CROSS Conference in Indianapolis. I was working at a booth and talking to students when I saw him enter with his wife, Bobbye. My wife and I went to greet them both and tell them how much we love them and miss seeing them. When we approached, he called us by name and asked specific questions about our ministry and how things were going. I walked away from that conversation with one more revelation from the Rankins. Of all the thousands of missionaries he led over the years, he remembered us. Why? Because he really loved us and all the others as well. He truly supported us, and his tenure with the IMB was evidence of that.

Some may disagree with policies or directions, but I don't think anyone who knew the Rankins could ever question their profound love and support for the missionaries they led around the world.

Mentoring strategies used:
- Modeling
- Supporting
- Confronting
- Correcting

How we spent time together: I haven't spent a lot of one-on-one time with Dr. Rankin. In fact, I think he would be surprised to know I think of him as a mentor. I sat under his teaching on numerous occasions, but the things that impacted me the most were how he interacted with others and how he led.

How I reproduce the investment: I am fiercely protective and loyal to those I mentor, and I teach my apprentices to never speak in a disparaging way about someone they are mentoring. The mentor-apprentice relationship is a very delicate and sacred bond. You can totally destroy it with just one off-handed comment.

TO THE NATIONS

Shepherd God's flock among you, not overseeing out of compulsion but freely, according to God's will; not for the money but eagerly; not lording it over those entrusted to you, but being examples to the flock. And when the chief Shepherd appears, you will receive the unfading crown of glory.

—1 Pet. 5:2–4

David Payne
Worthy Communication

Context: When I arrived in Peru in 1999, David and Judy Payne served as translators and linguists working on the Ashéninka language. They spent months with me, teaching me Ashéninka and helping me try to grasp the grammar. We worked together to develop Bible stories in the language, and I was privileged to distribute the fruit of their labors as I took Ashéninka New Testaments to the villages I was working in. As I took on the work with the Xtreme Team in 2005, what they taught me deeply affected how we trained our missionaries.

We had high expectations for our missionaries in regard to learning the mother tongue and ministering in that language. I think that is one of the major factors that made our team so successful in the places we worked. It is one of the best examples of how diverse mentors can increase wisdom and effectiveness. They never ceased to challenge me in regard to language, and they never allowed me to be lazy with my answers.

> J,
>
> *I want to take this opportunity to encourage you as you continue to pursue your missionary career. There are several things you should keep in mind. Our perspectives are different in regard to our missionary purpose. Yours is church planting, and mine is transmitting God's Word in people's heart language. Even though these perspectives are different, they certainly need each other to be successful.*
>
> *So here is a question I want you to consider: Can we actually say people have heard the gospel if they have not heard it in a language they can understand? In everything*

you do, keep that question in your consideration.

There will be opportunities to take the shortcut of doing things in a trade language, but, when possible, do your work in their native tongue. It will require more hard work from you and those you lead, but I am convinced it will be worth it in the end.

Never be lazy about language learning. The consequences of laziness in that part of your life are grave. They can even be eternal. I know you will strive for these things as you have here while working with me, but when the temptation comes to do things the easier way, remember my words to you.

On another note, I know you feel at home in the villages and with the people and that you would be content there probably for the rest of your life. But I want to encourage you to continue your educational endeavors. It may seem pointless now, but when you grow older and your responsibilities and influence grow, you will understand the need for further education. Your mind was given to you by God, and you should develop it in a way that would please Him.

I leave you with this quote from Uncle Cam: "The greatest missionary is the Bible in the mother tongue. It needs no furlough and is never considered a foreigner."

Your friend,
David Payne

Outcome of this letter on my life: The Paynes continued to be mentors and advisors to me throughout my time in South America until 2010. They challenged me to think outside of my organization's normal ethos of church planting and discipleship and go deeper. They challenged me to ask missiological questions I had not deeply considered.

Seeing people read or hear the scripture in their own language gave me a new perspective and helped me think outside my traditional missiological paradigm. Linguists are unique people. They see the world differently than the rest of us. They critique and analyze, and they seek true understanding. Then the best ones seek to pass that understanding on to others.

I think everyone would benefit from having a David Payne in their lives. I know I am eternally grateful for his investment in me.

Mentoring strategies used:
- Asking hard questions
- Offering wise counsel
- Giving responsibilities
- Coaching
- Encouraging excellence

How we spent time together: I spent a lot of time with David in the context of language learning. He was my best resource for understanding the Ashéninka language, and he spurred me on to learn more and more, to invest in people through their heart language. Then when it didn't go exactly as I had planned, he helped me figure out why and to try again.

In later years, he was my linguistic compass, always bringing me back to the heart language, even when the trade language was the easier road to travel. We would meet each other at a typical Peruvian restaurant, and as we talked about life and ministry, he would ask me all the *Why?* questions good mentors know how to ask. These questions caused me to search deeper into my strategy to look for motives. Was I doing something because it was best or because it was easiest? Sometimes I had the right answer, sometimes I didn't, but I relied on David to always ask those hard questions.

At the same time, I was learning about language, and David was learning from me and my team about a specific teaching methodology. So we modeled something very interesting: He was teaching me as his apprentice, but he also was learning from me. That requires a lot of humility and a strong desire for growth. In David's case, he just wanted whatever would help the Ashéninka understand and retain God's Word. I think that is what drove him.

How I reproduce the investment: I open myself up to learn from those I teach. I stress the importance of using the correct language for gospel proclamation and discipleship. I have not followed through on continuing my education yet. I hope to get to that someday soon.

> *Make every effort to supplement your faith with goodness, goodness with knowledge, knowledge with self-control, self-control with endurance, endurance with godliness, godliness with brotherly affection, and brotherly affection with love. For if these qualities are yours and are increasing, they will keep you from being useless or unfruitful in the knowledge of our Lord Jesus Christ.*
> —2 Pet. 1:5–8

CHAPTER 5
STARTING OVER

If I have seen further it is by standing on the shoulders of Giants.

—Isaac Newton

Tim Cearley
Tell Them about Jesus

Context: The year is 2015. After 10 years serving in the Amazon and the Andes, the Lord totally shocked my wife and me as He led us to move to Africa and begin a new team there, reaching out to the remote and unreached peoples in particularly difficult regions of the continent.

When we began hearing from the Lord about this big change, it seemed crazy. Susan and I were well-established in language, culture, and ministry in South America. We had a great team and felt fulfilled in our task.

But I think it was the familiarity that caused the Lord to shift us to another context. When you first start out in a strange land with a foreign language, you feel so inadequate. It is really scary. So you cry out to God. Those first few years on the field, you pray and read your Bible and study more than you ever have, mostly out of pure survival instinct.

But as time passes, you become more comfortable. You know the language and culture. You begin to figure out your job. And slowly, you begin to rely on your own understanding, and your reliance on the Lord often wanes a bit.

After 10 years in the same place, that was beginning to happen to me. And God in his ultimate wisdom rescued me by sending me to a new field where I would have to start all over—new language, new culture, new missionary community. I would have to rely on Him to survive this. I think that was His plan.

As I began pursuing this possibility, I was put in touch with Tim Cearley, our organization's leader for sub-Saharan Africa. To this day, I have never met a leader or mentor like Tim. He was unique in so many different ways, but my first impression of him was when we spoke on the phone. He was in South Africa; I was in Peru. Before we got off the phone, he said he would pray for me and for direction from the Lord. When I spoke to him again more than a month later, we revisited that conversation, and he told me he had prayed for me every day since we had talked, and I believed him. That wasn't some platitude. I knew he was *very* busy, and the idea that he had set aside time every day to pray for me and this big decision told me a lot about Tim Cearley.

For several years, I worked under Tim and many other great leaders in Africa. I saw his leadership through those who were leading me, and then for a short period of time, I worked directly under him, just before he retired. That short time confirmed some of the things I had observed from afar, and he stretched me in areas I had never excelled in before.

Hey, JT,

It seems that no sooner had we started working together that the Lord sent us on to a new task. As we depart from Africa, I encourage you to continue working hard at the task God has given you and lead those He has given you to grow in faith and love. The task is eternally important, but if your heart grows callused or cynical, all your hard work will be for nothing because it will be done through your flesh, not His Spirit. So don't neglect the things of the Spirit, and maintain a soft heart for the lost and hurting.

There is still a lot of work in these hard places. The people there desperately need to hear the good news of our Savior, Jesus. I know these places aren't easy to minister in, but don't be discouraged. Do whatever it takes to complete the task you were given. Color outside the lines, create new strategies, and cast a vision for the future. Keep pushing forward until the task is complete.

Never find yourself neglecting personal evangelism. It is important to keep our eyes on these fundamental tasks. Strategy is important, but if you are no longer sharing the gospel with the lost people in your life, you have forgotten the first things, the most important of all. One of the most uplifting and worshipful things you can do is tell someone about Jesus. If you are doing that in your personal life, it will give you the passion you need to develop strategy and vision for the lost of the nations.

As you build your teams, remember that a diverse team is the best team. You will need the wisdom of age and experience, but you also will need the enthusiasm and fresh ideas of youth. With such diversity, it is often difficult to form a consensus and for everyone to be on the same page. But it is your responsibility as a leader to cast the vision God has given you and help those you lead to get on the same page so their different gifts and skills can be used to accomplish His tasks.

Finally, I know you are a pretty serious guy. But don't take yourself too seriously. Laugh at yourself; don't be afraid to be silly when it is needed. Life is too short to be serious all the time.

I'm sure we will see each other again soon.

Tim Cearley

Outcome of this letter on my life: Tim's leadership was a fresh breeze to me. It was just what I needed to shock me out of my self-importance and help me remember to rely on the Lord, not my own abilities or wisdom.

He would say silly things that would make you shake your head, but he also demonstrated a passion for the nations and the courage to back up his passion. When he was expected to lead the continent from Johannesburg where language and culture were easy for him, he had the courage to step out and move into an unreached area of the continent and learn a language and reach out to his lost neighbors.

That wasn't an unexpected move, but it showed where his heart really was. He was not wrapped up in his position as much as he was wrapped up in his calling to take this message of hope and salvation and forgiveness of sin to the nations who are living in darkness. I'm thankful for Tim's leadership. He helped me get over myself.

Mentoring strategies used:
- Modeling
- Informal conversations
- Recommending and discussing books
- Debriefing decisions and ideas
- Encouragement

How we spent time together: We were often in meetings together, but the best times were when we sat in one of our homes, drinking chai tea and discussing what God was teaching us. Tim always seemed to go first, like he just couldn't wait to share what God was teaching him. He always told me about unbelievers with whom he had shared the gospel. He would ask about specific things going on with us and give us new things to think about.

How I reproduce the investment: Okay, brutal honesty: I'm still working on most of the things Tim taught me. I'm trying to live them out in my life before I pass them on to the next generation. I'll get there someday, but I'm not there yet.

> *Remember your leaders who have spoken God's word to you. As you carefully observe the outcome of their lives, imitate their faith.*
> —Heb. 13:7

Disclaimer

You are about to walk into a difficult stage of my life. In fact, although most of the wounds have healed, many of the scars are still tender. I really debated whether to include these chapters in the book. They reveal that even though I have been mentored by the best, I am still prone to lapses in judgment. I felt it was important to let you see the true picture of mentorship.

Mentorship does not produce perfect people. We still make mistakes and stumble along the way. But those who have mentors have someone to go to when they are hurt and struggling. Those mentors help them see things more clearly and not be blinded by hurt, emotion, or shame. They also help them respond properly to correction, hurt, or injury by guiding them in wisdom.

During times like this, we tend to let our emotions rule us. Imagine a small child trying to steer a car. They swerve all over the place as they react to every fear or perceived danger. They are more likely to hurt themselves or others, even in the most benign circumstances because their fear prevents them from perceiving the situation clearly. But if they are sitting on their father's lap and his hands are also on the wheel, it is fun, and they are able to manage the stress that comes at them.

That is the difference between going through a trial alone or with a mentor. In the following pages, you will see that there are times I was hurt, wanted to quit, and wanted to defend myself or blame others, but the presence of healthy mentors helped me steady my emotions and move forward in a healthier way.

STARTING OVER

Dr. Bob Calvert
Drive On

Context: One of the most difficult years of my life was 2017. While serving in Africa, I drank some alcohol in a way that caused a stumbling block to someone in my ministry context. I did not mean to be defiant or rebellious, but my actions were unwise, and I should have known better.

Let me be clear that I was not nor have I ever been drunk, and I was not behaving in a way that I personally believe was out of line with scripture. However, our organization had a strict policy; I broke that policy and underwent correction.

As a result, rumors started, and people slandered me and my ministry. They were the people we loved and cared for and served sacrificially. It was hard. I knew that what people were saying and thinking was not true, but I had no way to defend myself or tell my side of the story.

After investing so much in so many, we were greatly discouraged. It seemed like everyone believed the worst about us, and we were seriously considering not returning to the field. (We were stateside when all this went down.) I was angry, ashamed, betrayed, hurt, indignant, and defensive, as well as about 100 other conflicting emotions. I called on many friends for counsel; I received a lot. But Bob Calvert caught me at my lowest and was truly used by God to speak profound wisdom into my life. He helped me make a wise decision, and I am forever grateful.

> Hey, J,
>
> I'm sorry you are going through this, bud. I know it is difficult. I want to encourage you in the Lord, brother, and give you some counsel for what you should do next. I have

been in this game for a long time, man, and I have seen some stuff. I have watched you and your ministry and can attest to your character.

I know your intentions were not sinful or rebellious. But I think now, in hindsight, that you and I can agree that even godly men sometimes have lapses in judgment. That is what happened with you, but it's not the end of the world.

I know people are spreading untruths and you feel your name has been dragged through the mud and your reputation damaged. Let God handle your reputation, brother. You just keep being who you are. Live in forgiveness and passion. Trust the Lord for the days He has numbered for your life.

I know the temptation is to throw in the towel, to say forget these people, and to go out and serve the Lord without them. But that is your pride talking. I promise you: that would be a mistake.

Missionaries are usually good people, but they all have their flaws and blind spots. The only way to prove you are not who people say you are is to continue to live as you always have. Work hard, win the lost, plant churches, disciple men, and grow in your own walk with God. In time, people will know the truth, and you will have trusted God through a very painful and personal trial. But even if they never realize the truth, trust God and keep your eyes on Him. He will sort it all out in His time.

I love you, brother, and keep on doing the work He called you to.

Bob Calvert

Outcome of this letter on my life: Bob Calvert was just the right mix of experience, wisdom, and rebel that I needed. He gave me the exact kick in my butt I needed to get over my pride, but he also helped me accept my poor judgment and encouraged me to own it. I'd known Bob for years, but it was that one conversation that helped me see my present and future clearly and know how to manage both in a way that would glorify Christ.

Mentoring strategies used:
- Words of wisdom
- Confronting
- Encouraging

How we spent time together: I knew Bob for years, and I always enjoyed the stories he told around the dinner table. We were coworkers and friends. He had a lot of experience in Africa, and he helped me wrap my head around my new environment, but I would not have considered him a mentor.

When I was in my time of crisis, I began calling people I knew and trusted, asking for their thoughts and counsel. Many people supported me and encouraged me over the phone, but Bob started by confronting me. When he went down that road, I knew the conversation was going to be different, and I sat on the front porch as he helped me see things clearly and find a healthy path forward.

We are still friends, but I don't call on him regularly for counsel these days. God used one simple phone call and a wise friend to help me get my head on straight again.

How I reproduce the investment: I shoot straight with people I mentor. I tell them the hard facts, but I also try to help them find a healthy path forward like Bob did for me.

> *We urge you, brethren, admonish the unruly, encourage the fainthearted, help the weak, be patient with everyone.*
> —1 Thess. 5:14 NASB

Kevin Rodgers
Trusting Sovereignty

Context: In 2015, I had accepted a leadership role in Africa that required a lot of administrative responsibilities—not my strong point at all. So as I took on the role, and our leaders wisely chose Kevin Rodgers, who was currently doing the same job in another area, to mentor me in this new role. I thought he was going to help me with administrative tasks, but he ended up helping me with so much more.

For several months, he helped me adjust to the new job, but he was also always available for another perspective or even for counsel long after. Then came the turmoil of 2017. I did take the counsel of Bob Calvert, returned to the mission field, and got back to work.

We were no longer in a leadership position due to my breaching company policy. I had been in leadership for more than 12 years, so it was a bit of a hit to my pride. Honestly, I was still doubting God. Had we done the right thing by returning? I don't deserve this treatment.

Those thoughts were mostly on my mind, but I was just whining and complaining, being stubborn. I was so focused on my prideful struggles that I couldn't see what my God, the redeemer of people's mistakes, was doing right in front of me. Kevin helped me see things more clearly, consequently helping me stop my whining and get my head right.

Hey J,

> *Boy, we have really walked through some highs and lows together. I remember sitting in the truck while driving through Uganda as we hashed out our differences in style and leadership with transparency and blunt honesty. I remember how Tim Cearley squirmed in the back seat as we had*

one frank conversation after another. But I think both of us walked away with a greater understanding of and respect for one another after that trip. I am convinced that those types of conversations need to happen more often in our world.

There have been a lot of shake-ups and changes over the past couple of years. Some of those worked to your advantage, others played into your weaknesses. I know that where you are now is not where you expected or even wanted to be. But let me remind you of our Lord's sovereignty. He doesn't do things just because; He always has a purpose.

I know how driven and focused you are, and I think sometimes God might have to do something drastic to get your focus off something you are obsessing on to put you in the place where He wants to use you. I'm not sure you would have heard Him otherwise. But don't think that any of those traits or changes are beyond His control. He knows what He is doing, J. Trust him in that, and use your gifting where He has placed you for His service.

There are some other things you can take away from this that might help you move forward in leadership and grow in your walk with Him.

J, you are passionate and bold, but sometimes you lack balance. Learn to grow in those areas where you are lacking, and bring more balance to your leadership. Don't just rely on your strengths but also diligently work on your weaknesses. That will help you demonstrate the same leadership and humility both to those you lead and those who are in authority over you. It also will help you to not lead people into the same weaknesses and struggles you have had.

You are a nonconformist, dude; you push the boundaries and ask hard questions. I like that about you, but it also can be difficult for those in authority over you. You have to learn to work with them and help them see in you what I see in you. Don't give them dumb reasons to doubt or have misperceptions.

Don't allow those false perceptions or misunderstandings to persist just because you don't want to deal with your detractors. Show them the real you. Be humble but bold, driven but disciplined. Push the boundaries, but respect and honor those who made the boundary markers.

You are going to do great as you explore new possibilities in this missions landscape. I love you, brother, and I'm praying for you and those you lead.

Kevin

Outcome of this letter on my life: When Kevin and I met, we were peers, doing the same kind of work in different areas. God brought us together in a casual work relationship where we would see each other a few times a year. But I recognized Kevin's steady wisdom and his devotion to the people God had called him to minister to, and it won my respect.

When my great trial happened in 2017, I went to those I respected and to those I knew could give me good counsel because I wasn't sure what to do. Kevin spoke to me and encouraged me through the biggest trial I had ever encountered. He gave me wise counsel in a storm of emotions and damaged feelings. He helped me see God's purpose in the midst of my time of doubt. I now find myself thriving where God placed me—and much of that can be attributed to the wise words of Kevin Rodgers.

Mentoring strategies used:
- Encouragement
- Wise counsel
- Active listening
- Accountability

How we spent time together: Kevin and I have never lived close to each other. We would see each other at meetings sometimes, but when we were face-to-face, we would just catch up on the latest news in each other's lives. Most of the mentoring I have received from Kevin was in the form of e-mails and telephone conversations. He has always been available when I needed to ask for advice or have another opinion on something I was thinking through. One of his personal disciplines is answering e-mails, so I know if I write him, he will respond quickly. When you don't live nearby, you have to be creative in your communication.

How I reproduce the investment: I'm really working on "followship." I've always been a natural leader, but I have learned that a good leader must first become a good follower. Once again, I'm not there yet—working on it.

I also have fully embraced what God has for me during this season, and I tell the story regularly to those I mentor. Hopefully, they are not as stubborn as I am and will learn what God wants to teach them without such drastic measures.

> *And let us be concerned about one another in order to promote love and good works.*
> —Heb. 10:24

CHAPTER 6
THE MISSING CHAPTER: A DIFFICULT QUESTION

Context: As I was preparing the list of the most influential mentors throughout my life, I knew there were several I had to include. But about a year before I started writing this book, I got some news that shook me—and even now, I'm not 100 percent sure how to deal with it.

One of my mentors walked away from the faith. He is no longer walking in the way of God. I understand that he has resigned himself to agnosticism. I'm still not sure what to do with that. I remember so vividly as he walked alongside me as I was starting out as a missionary. He gave me wisdom and challenged my prideful ideas. I saw him demonstrate a deep love for a hurting people. I saw him lead his family and love everyone around him. But now it's gone.

Left in place of that leadership and faith are sorrow and pain. How could he, knowing the goodness of our God and knowing His love for the hurting, walk away and deny it had happened?

I don't have easy answers to that question, but I thought it would be dishonest to not write something about my friend and others you may know who influenced you greatly and then let you down.

I've thought a lot about this. The things he taught me were true. His current beliefs and behavior do not affect the integrity of the things he taught me, things like this:

- Love furiously. Love people until it hurts.
- Guard yourself against pride, and protect yourself from sexual immorality.
- Hard things are worth doing.

Over the decades, those precepts have proved to be true—even if their teacher failed to continue believing in them. But what do we do about those who have walked away? Well, we love them, and we pray for them. This letter is for those who have lost their way.

Dear Pilgrim,

I'm sorry we have not spoken in many years. Life has taken us both in different directions. But I have not forgotten the things you taught me and the investment you made in my life, and I want to share my gratitude with you for taking the time to pour into me and guide me in the way of God. Your guidance affected me and has affected many others through me.

I have heard the news that you no longer walk with God and have struck out onto a new path for your life. I know many challenges have come your way that have caused you to question. I know you have seen so much suffering. Some of those questions are so hard, if not impossible, to rectify from where we stand.

We can't understand how God would allow certain things or be silent during important moments. But remember, we are so very limited in our perspective. What we can see or imagine only spans the course of several years, but there is much more that cannot be seen from where we

THE MISSING CHAPTER: A DIFFICULT QUESTION

stand. I guess that is where faith comes in, and it seems that faith is in short supply these days.

I'm not writing this letter to try to convince you to return to God's way. I just want to tell you that in the midst of all of this, I love you, my dear Pilgrim. No matter what path you choose to take, what road you travel down, I love you. I pray you do not give yourself to bitterness or despair. Although you have closed the door to our Lord, I beg you not to lock it. In fact, it is my hope that you will leave the door cracked a bit and let Him take it from there. Jesus really loves you, Pilgrim, whether you choose to accept it or not.

I hope our paths cross very soon.

J

Outcome of this letter on my life: When it's personal, some questions are gut-wrenching. I totally understand those who would say he was never really a believer or he could not have walked away. But those people did not work alongside him or see him minister. They didn't see him physically suffer for the name of Christ. It's confusing. I don't have all the answers. I choose to believe that he, like all of us, is on a journey. He is currently taking a painful and treacherous detour. It seems easy because it is wide, and there are many people traveling that road. But we have seen the road signs, and they say that road leads to destruction. I pray that he will soon find his way back to the narrow path. It is difficult, and few sojourn on that trail—but it is the only one that leads to life.

CHAPTER 7
DEVELOPING A CULTURE OF MENTORSHIP

Here in Africa, my closet has become its own unique environment. If left unattended, the environment (darkness and dampness) of my closet has a major effect on its inhabitants (my clothes, shoes, and hats). Mold grows everywhere! Big, fuzzy, blue-green mold and black mold grow on everything in a matter of days. It is a natural process, dictated by a specific environment.

The good news is that I can control that environment to get the results I desire.

The same is true of our Christian environments. Left unattended, they often grow undesirable cultures. If we make holistic adjustments in the environment, however, we can nurture a healthy place where God can produce something beautiful in us, both individually and communally.

So how do we create a culture of mentorship as a church, small group, team, or organization? Unfortunately, it isn't as simple as reading a book or blog and following those instructions.

Think of my closet here in Africa. If I leave my boots or hat in the dark closet for a week, everything has a layer of mold growing on it when I return. Why? Because the closet is the perfect environment or culture for the mold to grow. So it really isn't about specific actions we take but about the culture we create.

If we create a culture conducive to mentorship, those things will happen organically. We often try to artificially create them when, actually, it is a natural process. Programs and plans usually only have a limited effect on the environment.

Imagine if I put a moisture-absorbing packet in my closet. It will work for a while, but eventually, the closet will devolve back to its natural state. So we have to open the door, let light in, and maybe remove some things so air can move. I have to change the environment completely so we can get our desired outcome.

So how do we create the proper environment for mentorship? It takes a lot of hard work, and first and foremost, it requires humility and a willingness to change.

Here are seven factors I have seen deeply impact a Christian environment so it becomes a culture where mentorship and disciple-making grow naturally.

- *Vulnerability:* This starts with the leaders. Be honest about your struggles, sins, and frustrations. Ask for help. Christian leaders should be vulnerable. Otherwise, darkness and pride create the opposite of what a Christian community should exemplify.
- *Confession:* Learn to confess your sins to one another. I have found that it actually exalts Christ. It reminds us that we are completely dependent on Him, and we never really arrive. We *need* Him, and we *need* our church to continue our growth. If you or others are not willing to admit when you are wrong, spiritual growth is sabotaged, and the community will reflect that.
- *Intense love of Jesus:* If we ever get sidetracked from our concentration on Jesus, the environment automatically changes.

If we start focusing our discussions on unworthy topics, the environment changes. But when we talk of Jesus, His teachings, God's Word, and more, we maintain our focus on the source of our transformation and growth.

- *Sacrificial love of the church:* That does not come naturally, but if you can nurture selflessness in the church, serve one another sacrificially, and put your brothers and sisters and their needs above your own, then God will teach you and teach the whole church through your example. Another result is that outsiders will notice. It is not in our human nature to put others first. The first-century church did it, and their contemporaries said, "Look…how they love one another…and how they are ready to die for each other."[2]
- *Community:* Eat meals together, study God's Word, and pray together. Live life together as the church, not just when you are assembled but always. It doesn't have to be some strange commune setting. Just be intentional about being the church with one another all throughout your week. Demonstrate a genuine love to be with God's people, and God will reveal Himself through those in your community.
- *Presence of elder Christians:* The elders are our guides. They have walked this narrow road for longer than the rest of us and have a desire to see you succeed and grow in Christ. Listen to their counsel as they point out the traps of false doctrine and unhealthy pursuits. The presence of elders will greatly affect the environment's health and speed of reproduction. Naturally, as we grow, we desire to be mature, and more elders and mentors are produced.

---

2. Tertullian, in "See How These Christians Love One Another," *Christian History Institute,* https://christianhistoryinstitute.org/magazine/article/see-how-these-christians-love.

- *Confrontation:* This is a difficult but necessary part of developing a culture where mentorship and disciple-making are normal. If you avoid confronting issues, spiritual growth will be impeded, and you will stagnate, giving sin a place to thrive. If mold grows on my boots and I just leave them alone, mold will grow even more. The mold has to be confronted to move forward. Confrontation in the church, however, has to be done in a loving, Christlike way because, as Paul said, you might be the one who needs grace the next time.

What Happens When That Environment Is Tampered With?

I recently observed a formerly healthy, growing community go down a very destructive path. I wondered what happened. I knew those people did not willingly go down this path. There were some new elements that came into the community, and previous healthy elements were removed. That changed the culture. As a result, the environment began developing new, less-desirable outcomes. Previously, they were unified, growing, confessing, and loving. But suspicion, unconfessed sin, jealousy, doubt, and deception came in. The enemy had the foothold he wanted, and much damage was done. We must be diligent and on guard, for our enemy takes great delight in the destruction of our unity, and he will do whatever he can to destroy us.

> *Flee from youthful passions, and pursue righteousness, faith, love, and peace, along with those who call on the Lord from a pure heart.*
> —2 Tim. 2:22

CHAPTER 8
DEAR PAUL: INVEST IN THE FUTURE

I usually recommend only mentored people to be mentors. But these days, fewer and fewer people have been mentored. I want to share with you 11 practices I would recommend that you develop as you begin to mentor others. It will help both you and your apprentice to have a more positive experience.

11 Things to Cultivate in Your Life If You Want to Be a Good Mentor

1. ***Personal follow-up:*** Make yourself available and take the time to sit down and have a conversation. If you talk about something important, be sure to follow up and see how your apprentices are doing and what progress they are making. This practice can really make or break a mentorship relationship, especially in the beginning.
2. ***Share things that inspire you:*** If you read or listen to something that impacts you, send a link to the ones you are mentoring. Buy them a book or an album, and then take the time to discuss it together.

3. ***Invest in people different than you:*** Our tendency is to surround ourselves with people who are like us, but try to find apprentices who are very different than you. It will amplify the things they learn, and it will also allow you to learn more during the process as their perspectives challenge you as well.
4. ***Practice clear and bold communication:*** You can't beat around the bush when mentoring. You have to address issues and do it in a loving way. Be sure you are communicating clearly as well. Think through your words; write them down, if necessary. Do whatever it takes to communicate clearly.
5. ***Pray for them and your relationship:*** If you are willing to commit to mentoring someone, you also must commit to praying for that person and devoting your relationship to the Lord. Ask God to draw you both closer to Him in the process of this mentorship.
6. ***Give assignments and tasks, and then debrief:*** Choose a challenging topic or passage of scripture or even a task that might be out of your apprentice's comfort zone. Let them try it, but you do it as well, and then debrief what you have both learned from the study or experience.
7. ***Model:*** Never teach something you are not willing to do yourself. Show your apprentice you are practicing what you preach. That may seem obvious, but you would be surprised how many mentors don't model the behavior they expect from their apprentices.
8. ***Speak hard truths but recognize that God is the one who transforms:*** Sometimes you will have to be blunt. Often, Christian love requires difficult conversations and even correction. But remember that your responsibility is to point them to Christ as He does His transforming work. It is not your job to punish or even change their behavior. You are just there to create the environment that allows them to hear from the Lord and be transformed by Him.

9. ***Don't forget to tell stories of your failures:*** This one is hard. Everyone likes telling good stories—you know, the ones that make us look good. But we usually learn more from our mistakes. So don't forget to give your apprentices the whole truth. Tell them about your mistakes and failures and how God used them for your good. Be humble and honest about your journey.
10. ***Passionately attack your weaknesses:*** I often ask people about what sin they are attacking in their lives. We should always be ready to quickly answer that question. If you have to think about it, you are likely not actively attacking sin in your life. But the mentor needs to share those things with the apprentice. They need to see you submitting to the Lord and killing sinful behaviors in your own life.
11. ***Set the standard high and watch them reach it:*** Have high expectations of those you mentor. Challenge them. When they are lazy, don't ignore it. We are training up the next generation. We cannot afford to make compromises, or we will fail them. In my experience, if you set the standard high, they will work harder and mature faster.

Things to Look for in an Apprentice

1. ***Doers, not knowers:*** Look for people who volunteer, who get involved, who already are trying to live out their faith in some way. Doers tend to be more focused on obedience to Jesus's teachings; knowers usually are more interested in just understanding for the sake of knowledge alone. Both knowledge and obedience are needed, and there must be a healthy balance. But those who are overbalanced on the knowledge side are difficult to mentor because their desires (knowledge) do not always align with the purpose for mentorship (character development).
2. ***God's choice:*** Sometimes the answer isn't as obvious as you might think. Sometimes we, like Samuel, look with hu-

man eyes and don't see what God sees in the hearts of our apprentices. So ask God to guide you to the right person. Sometimes He will surprise you with the person you might least expect.
3. ***Hunger for the Word:*** That can be demonstrated in multiple ways. Try to take a peek at your apprentice's Bible. If he or she is an older believer, you should see that the Bible is worn and written in. If he or she is a newer Christian and is asking a lot of good questions, it means that person is on the right track.
4. ***They recognize their struggles:*** Are your apprentices actively attacking sin in their lives? Are they able to openly discuss the things they are currently working on or want your help with?
5. ***A challenger:*** Look for someone who will challenge you to stay in the Word. You may not have the answers to all their questions, which will propel you into deeper study. The idea is that both of you are sharpening each other. Remember, iron sharpens iron. When you have a spiritually hungry apprentice, his or her hunger keeps you digging in the scripture for answers and wisdom. The situation becomes mutually beneficial.

Questions Mentors Should Ask When Starting a Mentor-Apprentice Relationship:

- What would you like to get out of this relationship?
- Why do you want to be mentored by me?
- What skills would you like to improve?
- Have you had mentors before?
- Who were your previous mentors?
- What did your previous mentors teach you?
- When and how often should we meet formally?

Topics You Should Regularly Discuss with Your Apprentice:
- Character
- Integrity
- Life skills
- Relationships
- Frustrations
- Joys and dreams
- Family

CHAPTER 9
DEAR TIMOTHY: CHOOSE WISELY

Becoming an apprentice is not usually as simple as finding someone to mentor you. Most good mentors have a line of people wanting to be mentored or discipled by them. But they have limited time, so they have to decide where to place their investment.

Your best bet, if you can find it, is to get involved with someone who is mentoring small groups of people. That allows for the best learning experience, and you can learn a lot from several different perspectives. That is what Jesus did with His disciples. They were learning from what Jesus said to them individually but also from what He did or said to other disciples who were present.

Even among the disciples, there were some who stuck out. Peter, James, and John were known as the inner circle because Jesus chose them. I think Jesus chose those three because they were serious about being mentored and sought a more profound experience. So Jesus invested more deeply in them. If you want that same experience, here are some tips to help you be a better apprentice.

Things to Cultivate in Yourself If You Want to Be an Apprentice

Pursue discipleship: Don't just wait for it to happen. If you desire to be mentored or discipled, you must actively pursue it. Ask questions to get your mentor's opinion on important decisions. Let your mentor challenge your ideas and theology. Ask them questions like these:
- How could I have done that better?
- What do you think about _____?
- What areas do you think I can improve in?
- What did you do in this season of your life?

If you permit your mentor to speak about the most sensitive areas of your life, you are opening yourself up to his or her guidance in ways most people prefer to avoid. Show your mentor you are serious. If you are willing to change your beliefs and behaviors, your mentor likely will be more inclined to invest in you.

Be teachable: This one is a must. If you are not teachable, you might as well give up now. If you think you already know everything you need to know and are almost always right, you will never be a good apprentice. You would be surprised how many apprentices go to their mentors with this attitude. Be teachable. Recognize that your mentor has experience that could be vitally important to you. Let your mentor guide you to make adjustments and see if his or her suggestions and direction help. If they do, explain how they helped you.

Read and discuss: If you are not already a reader, you should start. Develop your mind. Challenge yourself. Some people are more inclined to read than others. If you like to read or want to become a more prolific reader, get suggestions from your mentor. Read and discuss it with your mentor. If you are not a reader, that is no excuse. At least be an avid reader of the scripture and share regularly with your mentor what you are reading.

DEAR TIMOTHY: CHOOSE WISELY

Draw from many wells: I mentioned this in the introduction, but it is worth repeating. Seek multiple mentors from different backgrounds and different viewpoints. It's not always good to have only one mentor. Perhaps try to have mentors for various parts of your life. One may speak to your spiritual life and another to your professional or family life. There will be overlap, but diversity will help you be well-rounded.

Develop a watchful eye: Observe what your mentor does in different situations. Would you have done it the same way? Discover why your mentor does what he or she does. If you can't figure it out, ask politely. If you think you have figured it out, ask anyway, just to confirm. Be sure you are asking to learn why and not because you think you know a better way.

Be a helper: That applies especially to your mentor's family. Likely, your mentor will give up time with his or her family to mentor and disciple you. Pay your mentor back by helping out with something his or her family needs. Go to the store, babysit, run an errand, and more. Helping your mentor's family shows genuine love and helps his or her spouse and children know you and participate in your discipleship.

Learn to share interests: If your mentor likes country music, give it a try. If your mentor is into photography or art, see if he or she can teach you something. Those things create a bond and take an average mentorship to the next level. You might also learn something unexpected.

Find someone to mentor: Everyone should have a Paul and a Timothy in their lives—someone they are discipling and someone they are being discipled by. If you want your mentors to know you are serious, find an apprentice and start teaching them what you know and what you are learning from your mentor. That is how your mentor begins to take you seriously, and it will cause your mentor to be even more intentional in their discipleship of you because they know it is being passed on to the one you are mentoring. That is the most effective way to supercharge your mentorship—100 percent guaranteed.

Things to Look for in a Mentor

I have found that there are many people interested in being mentored. However, not everyone is going to be a good fit. Some people do not have the experience or ability; others don't have the time or energy. Here are 11 pointers to find a good mentor who will help you as you grow in your faith.

1. ***They talk about Jesus—a lot:*** Ultimately, you don't want to become like your mentor. You want them to help you become more like Jesus. For that to happen, you need to find someone who is in love with Jesus and whose relationship with Him guides their daily actions and character.
2. ***They have an awesome spouse:*** Often, people seem like a great mentor on the outside, but if their family life does not reflect the same leadership, you might want to think again. It is easy to lead in public, but if a mentor is not leading their spouse and family, they will likely disappoint you.
3. ***They value loyalty:*** How does a mentor talk about others? Do your best to find a mentor who values loyalty and refuses to speak poorly about those he or she leads or mentors. If someone is willing to talk bad about others, they will do the same with you.
4. ***They bring others to the table:*** Find someone who has many influences. If they are deeply involved in only one person's ministry or teaching, it will limit your growth. If someone is heavily influenced, for instance, by John Piper or John MacArthur but does not have other influences, the depth of your apprenticeship will be limited.

5. **Quick response time:** Many people say they are interested in mentoring, but when the realities and demands of mentoring hit them, they really don't have the time to fulfill the responsibility. If you contact them and they do not respond in a timely manner, it is likely they do not have the time to invest right now. Find someone else.
6. **They do one-on-one:** Mentoring groups can be a fulfilling experience. However, you want someone who is willing to do one-on-one as well. There are just some things you need to deal with in private.
7. **They have a contagious passion:** Seek someone who makes you feel passionate about living, reading scripture, sharing your faith, abiding in Christ, and so on. If they can pass that passion on to you, they can teach you how to pass it on to others as well.
8. **Their expertise is recognized by others:** How do others talk about your mentor? Do they recognize his or her abilities and character? Or do they wonder why you are considering that person as a mentor? Be careful if others don't see him or her in the same light as you do. Sometimes, others are simply wrong, but on the other hand, they may know something you don't know. Be careful.
9. **They have successfully mentored others:** Ask around to see if your mentor has ever mentored others. Find out if it was a good experience. Where are the others now? Do they now lead others? Are they leading healthy families? It might give you a good indication of the effect of this mentor.
10. **Constant eye contact (not distracted):** Eye contact is almost always a good test of someone's capacity as a mentor. When you are talking, are they looking at you, or are they working the room and looking around to see if there is anyone else they might want to talk to? If they cannot maintain eye contact with you in a busy room, they likely will not do well as a mentor.

11. ***Find a mentor who will ask you to do something that seems impossible:*** You want someone who will challenge you to do things you don't think you can do on your own. Perhaps it seems their standards are too high, but give it a shot. You might be surprised by how it turns out.

Questions Apprentices Should Ask

- How would you do _____?
- What areas can I improve in? Will you help me in that?
- What are my best traits and skills?
- What were some of the most important things your mentor taught you?
- How can I take things to the next level?
- What are some of the pitfalls you think I am susceptible to falling into?
- How do you _____?
- Who are some of your greatest influences?
- Who are the mentors you have had in your life?
- What author do you read the most?
- Who has been the biggest discouragement to you and why?
- What failures have you had in mentoring?
- Why do you want to mentor me?
- What do you see in me that you want to develop?
- Who is mentoring you right now?
- What new experience can you introduce me to?
- What are the greatest needs in the world today?
- Where should I start?
- What am I hiding from or closing myself off to?
- What have you learned this week?

CHAPTER 10
A STARTING POINT AND A PATH FORWARD

Writing the letters in this book was very enjoyable. I remembered fondly the influence of these men and women in my life. It was fun to remember them and the things they taught me.

It actually was pretty easy to write in their voice since most of their words are still bouncing around in my head. But mostly, it was a good reminder of how God has used others to influence my life. That inspires me to be intentional to do the same for others. So as we strive together to revive this ancient Christian practice of mentorship, let's take a look at some practical steps.

Unfortunately, you can't become a good mentor by reading a couple of best-selling books. Rather, the culture of mentorship is passed on organically. You are bearing fruit, passing on the spiritual DNA that was passed down to you. Those values have been grafted into who you are, and you bear that fruit naturally and (hopefully) abundantly. So where should you start?

First, you should find out where you are, recognize it, and develop and grow from there. See if these questions help.

Where Are You Now?

Who is your Paul? Have you ever had someone in your life who took you under their wing and invested time to guide you and walk with you through a stage of your Christian development?

If yes, answer these questions and take these actions:

- Who were they?

_____

_____

- What did they teach you?

_____

_____

- How did they mentor you?

_____

_____

- How have those things helped you in your life?

_____

_____

- Have you intentionally passed those teachings and life principles down to someone else? Who?

_____

_____

- Have you ever thanked your mentor for their investment in you?

_____

_____

- Sit down for a few moments now and write your mentor a letter. Tell them some things you learned from them. Tell them how you plan to pass those things on to the next generation. Honor them and their sacrificial love of you.

If no, answer these questions and take these actions:
- List five men or women you respect—people you would like to emulate because of their character and walk with God. Write out the reasons you admire them or the things you would like to learn from them. One or two mentors in your life is usually enough, but I encourage you to write five names because some of these men or women are going to be too busy to take you on, or they already are mentoring several others.

   1. _____
   2. _____
   3. _____
   4. _____
   5. _____

- Initiate contact. Write them a letter and tell them how you have seen God's hand in their life and how you would like to sit under their leadership and learn from them. If you don't like writing, invite them to coffee, and share these things face-to-face. The important thing is to ask if they will mentor you.

- Pursue mentorship. I love mentoring people, but my time is limited, and honestly, I normally only mentor those who pursue me in a mentor relationship. If they pursue it and don't give up, I will take time out of my day and spend it with them. But if it is just lip service and they don't ask for counsel or pursue my input, they usually fall through the cracks. So pursue it, write them, call them, and ask for advice and counsel. Look for their perspectives on life issues and passages of scripture, or share daily musings with them.

Who is your Timothy? Are you mentoring someone right now? Do you have a person in your life to whom you are passing on the important things others have taught you?

If yes, answer these questions and take these actions:

- Who are you currently mentoring?

___

- What are you trying to pass on to them?

___

- How are you intentionally training them up in these things?

___

- How can you make the mentor-apprentice relationship more vibrant and effective?

___

- Take a moment right now and write them a letter. Don't focus on what they still have to learn, but encourage them in the growth you have already seen in them. Inspire them to keep drawing closer to Christ. Spend time on this letter; it could very well be something they cherish their whole life.

A STARTING POINT AND A PATH FORWARD

If no, answer these questions and take these actions:

- Make a list of three people you know who show a lot of promise and in whom you would like to invest. Name three people because not everyone is open to the level of intimacy and vulnerability a mentor-apprentice relationship requires.

    1. _____
    2. _____
    3. _____

- Reach out to them and be clear about your desire to mentor them. Give them an idea of what it might look like—meeting for coffee and Bible study once a week, telephone calls during difficult decisions, meeting regularly to discuss or work through certain ideas or issues, and more.

    _____
    _____

- Be intentional in investing. Be the kind of mentor they will someday write a letter to. Work hard at it. Remember, Jesus's last instruction to us was to make disciples. That is exactly what He meant—taking time to make a disciple is hard work but very much worth the effort because the fruit is eternal.

    _____
    _____

Now that you know where you are and what lies ahead, I want to pass on one bit of information that I share with all those I have mentored over the years.

You Always Need a Paul and a Timothy in Your Life

You need to have someone who is investing in you (Paul) as well as someone you are investing in (Timothy). We often make the mistake of seeing that on a timeline. For the first years of our Christian walk, we are a Timothy until we are more mature and become a Paul. But God's kingdom does not work like that. If you don't have a Timothy, the investment of others stops with you, and you will miss out on the benefit of being sharpened by a younger brother or sister.

And if you ever get to a point that you think you only need a Timothy and no longer need a Paul in your life, you miss out on the wisdom you need for the next stage of your Christian growth. Even Paul said he had not yet reached or attained maturity. He had not moved past the point of needing a mentor. I cannot state this strongly enough: *You will always need mentors in your life!* You never get to a point where you outgrow mentorship. I will admit that as you mature, mentors are more difficult to find. But don't give up looking, and don't give in to pride that says you don't need one anymore.

I pray that you take this endeavor very seriously and devote yourself to being a mentor and an apprentice. I truly believe the future health of the church is dependent on relationships such as these.

> *Even when I am old and gray,*
> *God, do not abandon me.*
> *Then I will proclaim Your power*
> *to another generation,*
> *Your strength to all who are to come.*
>
> —Ps. 71:18

EPILOGUE

Where Are They Now?

Bill and Nadine Taliaferro: Bill has been a businessman for more than 40 years and has taught Sunday school classes and discipled people ever since I can remember. Nadine has been a nurse for more than 25 years and has spent her life serving her family, her church, and her patients. Today, they continue to work and pour into the ones God brings into their lives. They especially like pouring into their grandchildren and continuing the tradition of faith and the Christian legacy both sides of the family have enjoyed.

Dr. Jack Dale: Jack and his wife, Sherry, of 35 years now live in the Great Smoky Mountains of Tennessee where Jack is a school teacher. Jack continues to be faithful to each ministry opportunity God allows, whether it's serving students or furthering his education. Since 2004, Jack has devoted himself to mentoring the students God has placed in his classroom. He is always striving to lead those he works with and those he teaches into a deeper encounter with Jesus Christ. He also continues to use God's creation to teach people about their wonderful Creator.

Jeff Glenn: Jeff is still doing student work—35 years and still going strong. He is currently in Warner Robbins, Georgia, at Shirley Hills Baptist Church, teaching, preaching, discipling, mentoring, holding lock-ins, going on mission trips, and organizing youth camps. I don't know how he does it. I can't even imagine how many students he and his wife, Malea, have impacted. I am 100 percent sure I am just one story among many who have been deeply affected by their faithfulness and example.

Jesse Fletcher: Someday, a biography will be written about Dr. Fletcher. It would take a whole book to tell you about the things he did in his life. In 1964, he helped start the Journeyman program for the International Mission Board of the Southern Baptist Convention. I served in this program from 1999–2001. He also served as the president, chancellor, and president emeritus of Hardin-Simmons University, which I attended from 1994–1998. He was also a recognized oil painter, focusing his craft on the beautiful West Texas landscapes.

In his lifetime, he published 12 books, including *Bill Wallace of China*, *Practical Discipleship*, *Living Sacrifices: A Missionary Odyssey*, *The Southern Baptist Convention: A Sesquicentennial History*, *The Wimpy Harper Story*, and *The Mission of the Church*.

He quietly ministered to people in Abilene, Texas, from every background and creed, demonstrating to them the love of Christ in the most tangible ways. He discipled countless church leaders, students, and missionaries in his 86 years of life and ministry.

Dr. Fletcher cared for his wife, Dorothy, until 2013, when she passed into eternity. He resided in Abilene, Texas, until his passing in 2018, no doubt ministering to the residents and workers there until the end. Jesse's son, Scott, said this about his dad: "He truly loves God with all of his heart, and he allowed that love to carve his path in the world." What else can we hope for?

EPILOGUE

James Shields: Dr. Shields still lives in Abilene, Texas, with his wife, Corrine, to whom he has been married for 65 years. He was a professor at Howard Payne University and Hardin-Simmons University for 40 years altogether. Although he has now been retired for almost 20 years, he continues to serve, mentor, and minister to those around him. He has been battling cancer for years, but you would never know it by talking to him. He continues to be faithful in his tasks as a husband, father, and mentor. Over the years, Dr. Shields has done almost 70 interim pastorates for churches, offering stability for those church bodies during a difficult transition time and helping them focus on the next steps and how God might use them in the future. Howard Payne University has a scholarship fund in the name of James and Corrine Shields. If you would like to give in his honor, you can contact them at hputx.edu.

Linda Carleton: In 2004, Linda Carleton, dean of Hardin-Simmons University, helped pilot a community outreach program in Abilene, Texas, that later became a nonprofit called Connecting Caring Communities (wecareabilene.org). She retired in 2008 from the university but continued to serve on the board of the nonprofit until 2015.

She has continued to actively mentor in her local church, loving on young families and discipling other women in the church. She and her husband, Rob, also spend a lot of time pouring into the next generation and securing their godly legacy by being there for their grandchildren and supporting them in their endeavors.

Chris Ammons: After leaving Peru, Chris and his wife, Pam, served as theological educators for rural pastors in Thailand, Myanmar, Cambodia, and Pakistan. Then they returned to the Americas to finish out their 29 years with the International Mission Board in Oaxaca, Mexico, training and mentoring national workers. They have served for many years fulfilling the Great Commission and making disciples wherever they go. They mentored many young families and singles to follow their example of faithfulness to the task. Chris is currently serving as the pastor of Silver Spring Baptist Church in Columbia, Pennsylvania.

Avery Willis: Avery passed on in July 2010 after battling leukemia for seven months. He has now entered eternity, but the work he did while on earth will continue bearing fruit for a long time to come. Avery served in Indonesia for 14 years with the International Mission Board and then served in an executive position for 11 years. He also served 15 years with Lifeway Christian Resources.

He wrote the MasterLife discipleship series and *The Biblical Basis of Missions*. He helped develop audio recordings of 400 Bible stories and was instrumental in organizing the International Orality Network. His impact was felt both on a personal level by those who knew him and on a much larger spectrum as his work and writings impacted people around the world. MasterLife has been translated into more than 50 languages and used in more than 100 countries.

Steve King: Life on the mission field took its toll on Steve's body, and when he returned from the field, he suffered multiple health issues that restricted his travel for years. Once his health stabilized, he became the minister of discipleship and evangelism at Friendly Avenue Baptist Church in Greensboro, North Carolina, where he has been used by God to ignite a passion in the church for the deeper life and for sharpening each other in the Word. The area where God has placed Steve to minister and mentor is one of the most unreached areas in all of North Carolina, and he continues building God's kingdom there by making disciples who make disciples.

Randy Griffin: Randy worked for 34 years with the Kern County Fire Department and the last five years with a Type One Crew in which he focused on mentoring young men not only in firefighting

EPILOGUE

but also in what it means to be a good man. He served on mission trips to Peru, Mexico, Brazil, Rwanda, and Uganda. He helped start a Hispanic church in Bakersfield, California, and taught a Sunday school class there for years. He also worked with the homeless and addicts in his local community. He has continued to learn and conquer new challenges and has recently become proficient in welding and metal work. He is learning jujitsu and continues to cycle and work out. In 2014, he and his wife, Cyd, moved to Washington State to fulfill his lifelong dream of living in the mountains, salmon fishing in his own backyard, and working in his shop. He and Cyd have continued to be involved with what God is doing around the world by serving with Vineyard Christian School in Rwanda, being active in his local church, and leading a Bible study for his neighbors. He also has four amazing grandchildren that benefit from his love and leadership.

Jerry Rankin: Jerry served as president of the IMB for 17 years after serving as a missionary in Indonesia for 23 years. He retired in 2010. Since then, he has been active in many ways, most recently by teaching evangelism and mission courses at his alma mater, Mississippi College in Clinton, Mississippi. He also directs the Zwemer Center for Muslim Studies at Columbia International University in Columbia, South Carolina, and serves on that institution's board.

Over the years, he has written seven books: *A Journey of Faith and Sacrifice: Retracing the Steps of Lottie Moon, To the Ends of the Earth: Empowering Kingdom Growth, Lives Given, Not Taken: 21st Century Southern Baptist Martyrs, The Challenge to Great Commission Obedience: Motivational Messages for Contemporary Missionaries, Spiritual Warfare: The Battle for God's Glory, In the Secret Place: A Pilgrimage through the Psalms,* and *Spiritual Warfare and Missions: The Battle for God's Glory among the Nations.*

David Payne: David and his wife, Judy, have retired from Wycliffe Bible Translators, but they are still actively involved in the work with the Ashéninka people. They have finished the draft of the entire Bible (Old and New Testaments) in the Ashéninka language, and they now do discipleship in 13 villages in the mother tongue of the Ashéninka people, giving them access to deep spiritual truths that can only be fully understood in their own language. David and Judy and many other translators and linguists are the unsung heroes of the missions world.

Tim Cearley: Tim and his wife, Charlotte, went to Zimbabwe in 1983 and retired after living in five countries and serving 35 years as missionaries. After retirement, Tim colored outside the lines by pursuing evangelism and discipleship in the most creative places. He worked at the YMCA and as an Uber driver. (I wonder how many gospel presentations happened in that car!) He is now the community ministries director of the First Baptist Church in Montgomery, Alabama, where he continues to reach out to the nations by ministering to internationals, working in the inner city with disadvantaged people. He and Charlotte are right in the middle of the need so they can shine the light of Jesus for all to see. No one will ever accuse them of hiding their light under a bushel.

Dr. Bob Calvert: Bob and his wife, Nancy, retired from our organization in 2015, returning to Arkansas to be with ailing parents. After both of his parents passed, Bob and Nancy moved to Sumter, South Carolina, to work as the minister of senior adults, missions, and evangelism at First Baptist Church. They call him the "visiting pastor" since much of his time is spent visiting people in some of their most difficult times of need. He also is leading ministries to internationals living in the United States and taking groups on mission trips every year. As Bob would say, "He is busier than a one-legged cat in a litter box." But I think that's kind of the way he likes it.

Kevin Rodgers: After serving in Zambia for 19 years, Kevin moved to Kenya in 2016 to continue serving the Lord in a similar leadership

EPILOGUE

role but in a different language and cultural context. He also took on the leadership of the theological education of all sub-Saharan Africa. Currently, he is preaching in local churches almost every Sunday. He mentors and trains every missionary who comes to work in sub-Saharan Africa through 20/20, a training program he developed. He also is actively discipling national believers and missionaries under his leadership, preparing the next generation to make disciples throughout the continent of Africa and beyond.

I have not written about all the men and women who have mentored and influenced me. There are many more than the ones I mentioned in this book. I have just tried to choose some important stories from different stages of my journey. I have not mentioned Finis Christenberry, who showed me what a true elder looks like, or James Eades, who taught me how to include children in the kingdom work. I didn't mention David Crane, who taught me so much about Africa, or Andy Caperton, who taught me about humility. There are so many more. I hope you will be as blessed as I have been by the men and women God has placed in my life.

ACKNOWLEDGMENTS

First, I want to thank my amazing wife and helpmate, Susan. You are so perfectly matched to me. You have been my constant advocate and encouragement. You've been by my side when everything looked very grim but also when we felt blessed beyond measure. In fact, you are my greatest gift and blessing from the Lord.

To my children, Victory, Memphis, Ember, and Daniel, thank you for sacrificing time with Daddy to let me write this book. I know you were wondering what in the world I was doing, but I hope this book can be useful for you, too, someday.

Mom and Dad, thanks for never giving up on me. You always demonstrated unconditional love since the day I was born and sound counsel since I was old enough to listen.

Georgia Reed, thanks for looking over the first and ugliest version of this book, giving me insight and encouraging me to keep going.

Curt Iles, thanks for being the first "real author" to read my book. On a road trip through the bush of Northern Uganda, your encouragement helped me make it through the final push of writing necessary to make this book a reality.

Mark Kelly, your experience and guidance were essential to this whole process. You helped me refine my book, but you also forced me to think about the big picture and the entire writing and publishing process.

Thanks to Lucid Books for believing in me and giving me a shot. Thanks especially to Megan Poling, who walked with me through this process from the beginning, and also the proofreaders, graphic artists, and everyone else involved.

To my friends, teammates, mentors, and apprentices in the International Mission Board, thank you for inspiring me, challenging me to grow, and allowing me to experience life on the edge of eternity.

To the Ashéninka team, thanks for introducing me to a life of following Jesus into impossible places and letting me see the hand of God at work in and through humble vessels.

To the Xtreme Team, you guys took it to the next level. It was a pleasure to lead you, and you inspired me to be a better strategist and mentor. Your hard work and dedication helped me see the scope of influence God can have through people who the world has deemed too young or too wild.

To the Echelon Team, you will always be my family. You stood with me when I felt abandoned. Against all odds (and with bullets flying), we expanded His kingdom while growing in love for one another and the people we served.

To the Borderlands Team, just when I had gotten comfortable, God took me into a world that I knew absolutely nothing about. Each of you has been encouragers and friends during this crazy transition. I have learned so much from you, and I look forward to seeing how God uses you in years to come. Chris Willis, thanks for your very personal support of this book.

I had 15 phenomenal beta readers who honed my focus and clarified my words. I especially want to thank Linzi Cole, Madelyn Phillips, Greg Bowman, Scott Corrao, and Michael Seger for never missing an opportunity to give me helpful input and refining my ideas into something publishable.

To my Launch Team, thanks for helping me see things from my readers' perspectives and, most of all, for sharing this book with your circles of influence.

ACKNOWLEDGMENTS

To the mentors I wrote about in this book and the others I did not mention but who have invested in me and given sacrificially of themselves, thank you.

I want to thank Alejo and Americo who taught me about obedience and hospitality while I was in the jungle.

For Teko Simon, I'm very proud of the godly man you have become.

To Nasser Edin, your perseverance and love of the true gospel is always an inspiration to me.

And finally, Jonathan Williams, you were my champion when I first started writing. You have continued to support and encourage me to this day, and I will forever be grateful for your kindness and example.

CPSIA information can be obtained
at www.ICGtesting.com
Printed in the USA
BVHW040330150820
586431BV00007B/374